Fundamentals of Dressage

Fundamentals of Dressage

Alfred Knopfhart

Translated by Nicole Bartle

J. A. Allen
London

British Library Cataloguing in Publication Data

Knopfhart, Alfred
    Fundamentals of dressage.
    1. Livestock: Horses. Riding. Dressage
    I. Title II. Grundlagen des Dressurreitens. *English*
    798.2'3

    ISBN 0-85131-494-5

First published in Germany as *Grundlagen des Dressurreitens*
© 1979 Verlagsbuchhandlung, Paul Parey, Berlin and Hamburg

English translation © J. A. Allen, 1990

Published in Great Britain in 1990 by
J. A. Allen & Company Limited
1, Lower Grosvenor Place
London SW1W 0EL

Book production Bill Ireson
Typeset by Waveney Typesetters, Norwich
Printed in Great Britain by
St Edmundsbury Press Ltd, Bury St Edmunds, Suffolk

Contents

List of Illustrations

Introduction

This book is intended for riders, trainers, teachers and judges of dressage. It presents a method of educating horses up to the level of Grand Prix dressage, sets out contemporary criteria of correctness and suggests ways of improving performance and correcting faults.

It should however be made clear that the various movements described and demanded in tests are not the object of dressage. It must be borne in mind that the point of dressage is to develop the natural aptitudes of horses, their strength, suppleness and agility, to generally improve their gaits and make them more pleasant to ride.

The various movements prescribed in tests are only a means to that end. Dressage will have failed in its purpose if the horse's natural carriage and movement, instead of improving, has deteriorated as a result of unenlightened and hasty methods of schooling.

What judges should look for is a work of equestrian art, simply a perfectly tractable horse that moves with total ease and with consummate fluency and elegance at all speeds. Minor inaccuracies in the execution of some lessons are less important than beauty or purity of movement.

Some of the succeeding chapters have already appeared in specialized equestrian journals in Germany and abroad and have been so favourably commented on by acknowledged dressage authorities that I have been encouraged to put them together in slightly more elaborate form.

Alfred Knopfhart, Laxenburg

PART ONE
Explanation of the Concepts of Dressage

1 Purity of Movement

The dressage judge frequently gets the impression that the high aspirations of the riders are not always matched by a clear understanding of the purpose of dressage. This may be because there still exists amongst judges at national or international venues a certain difference of views on points of detail, but criticism of the present system of judging and comparing performance is beyond the scope of this book which is meant to explain as concisely as possible the essential requirements, the *sine qua non* of dressage; nevertheless one thing is certain and that is that all judges agree that the first and foremost requirement is *purity of movement*.

It is regrettable that not all horsemen speak the same language; words mean one thing to some and a different thing to others. It has always been so and has always led to heated argument. Purity of movement, suppleness, impulsion, rein tension, elevation, etc. are notions which are only vaguely understood but none more than 'purity of movement'. Some riders understand that it means regular sequence of steps; others believe that it means equal distribution of weight over all four legs, or, more simply, that a horse is sound in all its limbs, or at least shows no obvious sign of lameness. Neither of them show a perfect understanding of the concept. Correct sequence and regularity of steps are certainly requisites of purity of movement, but the term implies the horse's whole way of going, not only the movements of its limbs.

A horse sets itself in motion by pushing its mass

Purity of gait. Everything flowing and in supple impulsion ('Schwung').
The rider sits with a supple seat and 'lets the movement out'

forwards with its hind limbs until its centre of gravity
moves beyond the base of support covered by its four
limbs. Since horses, like all earthly bodies, are subject to
the laws of gravity, the result of the displacement of the
centre of gravity beyond the base of support is a
temporary loss of stability; the horse must advance a fore
limb to preserve the equilibrium of forces. The rider of
course need not worry about the principles of motion;
what should concern him is not the fact of movement but
the way in which the horse moves – not the 'why' or the
'what' but the 'how'.

What purity of movement really implies is: regularity of
movement of the limbs; engagement of the hind legs,
smooth, elastic activity of all the joints and muscles of the
hindquarters; activity of the back muscles; freedom of
movement of the shoulders; elevation of the neck and

The horse tenses up into a 'defensive position'. There is resistance in the poll, the back is 'dead', and the hind legs lack activity

head; steady, relaxed head carriage; quiet chewing of the bit, variable applications of even tension on the reins. The elegantly arched and quietly swinging tail completes the picture. Rhythm, suppleness, carriage, equilibrium, straightness, impulsion and submission (of a degree commensurate with the degree of education of the horse) are all essential elements of purity of movement.

Therefore, even if the timing of the footfalls is regular, the movement cannot be said to be pure if it is sluggish or hurried, if the back muscles are inactive, if the head is rigidly set, if the horse is not on the bit. How can the reins fulfil their principal function, which is to control the hindquarters, if their effect stops at the poll or at the withers, or if the horse resists them by stiffening or slackening its back muscles? The other aids will then be just as ineffective.

Flawless performance of a test is inconceivable if the movement is not absolutely pure at all gaits and all speeds. Purity of movement in fact means the same thing as grace, efficiency, suppleness or ease of movement. A dressage horse should move without apparent effort, which does not mean without energy; it is as we say 'in front of the leg', meaning that it goes forwards spontaneously, without having to be urged on at every step by the rider; it does not weigh on the hand; it uses the muscles of its back and hindquarters to dampen the jolts of locomotion so that its supple rider can sit comfortably and use the aids with discretion. The results of purity of movement are the smoothness of the ride and the elastic rein tension, permitting stillness of hands, close, easy contact of legs, and nuance in the application of the aids, all things which go to make the horse look even more beautiful than nature has made it.

The most important condition of purity of movement, however, is the suppleness and independence of the seat of the rider. A horse cannot move with ease and perform at its best if the way the rider sits causes it discomfort. Sooner or later, the purity of movement of even a well-schooled horse will be destroyed by a rider who hangs on to the reins, who has to grip, who hits the saddle hard at every step of the trot; the more sensitive the horse, the more it will stiffen. The more it stiffens, the higher it bounces the rider who then has to grip even harder to prevent himself becoming completely dislodged. Under those conditions, still and sensitive hands, relative but always even rein tension, are impossible. It is a vicious circle for which there is no other remedy except learning to sit correctly, learning to go with the movement and to feel the movement of the horse.

Purity of movement does not, therefore, depend only on the horse; it can be purchased but it has to be preserved.

If the rider is incapable of doing so, his prospects of success in competition, at any level, will remain pretty dim. But many of my fellow judges feel, as I do, that riders generally are more interested in the exact execution of the movements prescribed in the tests than with their manner of sitting and their horse's manner of going. They ride a test as if it was just a matter of proceeding from one place to another, from letter to letter, as if these were stations of the Golgotha. They think more about what to do than how to do it.

Purity of movement may be desirable but is not essential in show-jumping. The important thing in show-jumping is to clear the obstacles in the shortest possible time, and the show-jumping rider would rather beat the clock with a horse that canters disunited, than be left out of the running with one that moves stylishly but will not be hurried. Dressage is a different discipline; the movements prescribed are not like obstacles that have to be surmounted even at the cost of grace. A dressage horse that moves fluently at all gaits can be forgiven the occasional insignificant bungling of a movement and should have a better chance of being placed close to the top than one who executes all the movements with accuracy but with a certain lack of grace. Unfortunately inaccuracy is much easier to note than impurity of movement and is usually noticed not only by the judges, but also by the spectators.

However, in practice, purity of movement and accuracy go together. I have laboured the point only to stress the greater importance of purity of movement, but a properly educated horse will execute the movements accurately and without difficulty for the very reason that it moves easily and is docile, leaving its rider free to concentrate on speed and direction. On the contrary, a horse that does not move correctly, though it may execute most of the movements

Natural carriage of a young horse of good conformation

at the right place will not be able to execute fluently some of the difficult ones (for example the rein-back and the flying changes of canter).

Accuracy is not proof of purity of movement. For example, a walk-pirouette that starts and finishes at the prescribed spot does not prove the purity of the walk; a passage may be regular but is of little value if the collected trot is not lively or the extended trot long-reaching; flying changes, the half-pass at canter and the canter-pirouette can be executed by a horse that canters four-time.

Carriage of a mounted horse in the transitional period of education towards collection

The piaffer is the exception. A fluent transition to and from piaffer, a tendency to move forwards during the execution of the movement, on a light but constant tension of the reins is a clear demonstration of purity of movement.

A horse that normally moves with grace and fluency could be a little hesitant in a particular test that is new to it, but may still be more correct in its movement than another that has been so thoroughly rehearsed that it can be practically left to reel off the test like an automaton.

It is necessary to prescribe movements for tests at various levels to show that a horse is sufficiently advanced in its education. The movements are the lessons the horse has had to learn, parts of the curriculum for each stage of its education; but learning lessons is not the object of education. The various movements are simply exercises devised to improve the elements of correct movement: impulsion, suppleness, straightness, submission, collection. Judges, trainers, riders and spectators must always bear in mind that the sole purpose of dressage is the

Natural equilibrium of an unmounted horse moving in hand at a free and easy trot

Trot in perfect diagonals of a ridden horse in acquired equilibrium. The rider shows an exemplary deepness of seat

production of a totally amenable horse that carries itself freely in perfect balance in all three gaits, that can be easily collected or extended, and can go for hours without fatiguing its rider.

2 Rhythm, Speed, Carriage

As I said earlier, all horsemen unfortunately do not speak the same language, and I must therefore explain the meaning of certain words of the German vocabulary of dressage.

For rhythm, we say tact, a word borrowed from the language of music, meaning a stroke in beating time. For speed, we say tempo, which in music, means the rate at which a piece is meant to be played; in horsemanship it simply means degree of speed in moving from one place to another.

To satisfy the requirements of purity of movement, although a horse's speed or tempo may be changed by changing gait or by lengthening or shortening the strides, tact (beat or rhythm) must always remain perfectly regular. There must always be four distinct beats or footfalls, separated by an equal measure of time, to each stride of a correct walk; two distinct beats to a stride at the trot and three at the canter.

In dressage, regularity of beat is an absolute requisite for correct movement; until this has been perfectly established on straight lines and circles on one track the horse should not be taught any more difficult movements.

And now to carriage. Carriage means the manner in which the horse holds its head and whole body in relation to the base of support; it does not refer only to the position of head and neck. Correct carriage is a determinant of and also a result of equilibrium, balance, and speed.

To allow a horse to safeguard its balance in motion, its

centre of gravity must remain within (but not necessarily exactly above the centre of) its base of support and – for reasons which may not be immediately evident – elasticity of the poll is a very important condition of control of speed and balance.

It is at the working trot that we first teach the horse to carry itself. The working trot is rarely the normal trot of a horse; it is developed from the normal trot on the lightest possible contact which is used during the period of breaking-in to accustom the horse to the presence of the rider. The working trot has a determined rhythm which should be known by the rider; since the natural trot of the horse is usually too slow, too hurried, or irregular. To obtain the working trot the rider has to regulate the movement with either hands or legs and the rein tension must become more positive than a mere contact. The rider must get the horse to work energetically at a regular rhythm and at a steady but brisk speed, picking up its feet, flexing and extending smoothly and equally all the joints of the hindquarters. It must eventually learn to maintain the speed of its own accord. The movements of its limbs must gradually become rounder, more expansive and its trot easier to sit to.

Most importantly, the weight has to be distributed equally over all four legs; each leg must be equally loaded, so that none wears out sooner than the others. The hind feet must therefore be made to engage, that is to advance sufficiently to relieve the forelegs of an excess of weight, but greater engagement of hocks, pronounced flexion of haunches, lightness of the forehand, elevation of head and neck must not be demanded; they belong to a much later stage of schooling.

The working trot is easily obtained from horses with outstandingly favourable mental and physical aptitudes; such horses are not easy to find and are understandably

Increase of speed by correct extension of the trot. Lengthened outline, active back muscles, distinct footfalls, rider sitting deep and going with the movement

very expensive. With the majority of horses patience and skill are needed to develop it.

It is at the walk, with its eight phases of movement (each foreleg and hind leg alternately pushing, reaching forwards and supporting) that irregularity is most obvious. One leg may be weaker or stronger than the other three and come into support too soon or too late. Hind feet may drag and forefeet stamp. (One must be warned however against the optical illusion produced by limbs of uneven coloration.) All those irregularities have to be corrected, but at the beginning of schooling the walk should only be used to let the horse unwind between periods of trotting.

Exaggerated and incorrect extension of the trot. Excessive propulsion and insufficient support from the hind legs; the horse is 'running', overbent and has too much weight on the forehand

The importance of absolute regularity of beat is one of the reasons for the particular difficulty of the discipline of dressage. Long experience of observing horses and especially of riding many different ones is required to train the senses of sight and balance to recognize immediately the slightest irregularity of movement. A rider with a poorly developed sense of balance will never be able to develop the sense of balance of the horse.

3 Equilibrium

A body is in perfectly stable equilibrium when its centre of gravity is located exactly above the centre of its base of support. It can still preserve balance if its centre of gravity stays within its base of support, even if it is not situated exactly above the centre of the area of support. If the centre of gravity moves outside the base of support, equilibrium becomes unstable and a movement has to be made to restore stability. The smaller the base of support relative to the size of the body, the quicker a new base of support has to be established. A perfect sphere is a typical example of this principle: centre of motion and centre of gravity are coincident and in line with the base of support; the sphere will start rolling at the slightest displacement of the centre of gravity.

A horse with a long base of support, what we call a 'rectangular horse', is a safer, easier horse to ride than a horse with a short base of support, a 'square horse'.

At the halt, the base of support of the horse is the space covered by its four feet. To satisfy the conditions of perfectly stable equilibrium, the same amount of weight would have to be carried by each leg and the centre of gravity would have to be above the centre of the base of support. However in the horse, the centre of gravity is closer to the forelegs than the hind legs, therefore, at the halt, the forelegs are more loaded than the hind legs, but, as previously pointed out, equilibrium is stable if the centre of gravity stays within the base of support. The forward position of the centre of gravity favours momentum and this fact is exploited by the modern race jockey who can poise himself above the centre of gravity of his steed. But the dressage rider would be at a considerable mechanical disadvantage if he were poised above the centre of gravity of the horse. Moreover he is less interested in speed than manoeuvrability and so he sits above the centre of motion of the horse, not above the centre of gravity.

To be ready to change instantly its state of motion, the horse has to modify the state of equilibrium that allows it to stand at rest.

The forelegs of the horse contribute little to the production of forward movement; they act mainly to restore stability of equilibrium after displacement of the centre of gravity by the thrust of the hind legs. The hind legs on the other hand are jointed levers for the production of forward movement and are not really designed to carry a preponderance of weight (although at liberty excited stallions will prance with head and neck elevated and most of their weight on their hind legs).

The forelegs are also less efficient as shock absorbers than the hind legs because of the straight alignment of the forearm and cannon bones during the phase of support of their movement.

When it has to carry the weight of a rider, an untrained horse will overload its forelegs and will very soon damage them if it is not educated to redistribute the weight more equally over all four limbs. The rider must therefore get the horse to engage its hind legs, that is to advance them sufficiently in the direction of the centre of gravity so that it can use them not only to propel itself forwards, but also to relieve the forelegs of an excess of weight. Gradually the horse has to learn to move in 'horizontal equilibrium', that is with the weight equally distributed over fore and hind limbs.

Hind feet insufficiently engaged and not therefore supporting enough weight. Although the outline is fairly pleasing, the horse is on the forehand, and the rider is perched on the horse

At a later stage of its education, the horse will progressively also have to learn to collect itself, to engage its hocks, to flex its haunches and lighten its shoulders even more by lowering its croup. The flexion of haunches allows a 'relative elevation' of head and neck. In fact, the very collected movements of the High School included nowadays in advanced dressage, piaffer and passage, demanding extreme flexion of haunches, were originally meant to be just *lessons* designed to develop as much as possible the carrying capacity of the hindquarters in preparation for the airs above the ground of the High School.

But first the horse must learn to move in horizontal equilibrium; the rider must never attempt to collect it before this horizontal equilibrium is perfectly confirmed and the strength of the hindquarters has been sufficiently developed to start asking them to carry a preponderance of weight. Once horizontal equilibrium is confirmed, collection, which involves increased loading of the hindquarters, can then be produced – but only very gradually – by the systematic practice of certain gymnastic lessons designed to develop their carrying capacity. If an impatient rider tried to gather his horse too soon he would provoke resistance; even a normally calm and willing horse can be driven to exasperation by excessive demands. It is impossible to obtain by force an engagement of hocks and flexion of haunches that would cause a horse pain. Nothing can be more dangerous than using the reins to utilize the neck as a lever to enforce the flexion of haunches if the muscles of the back and hindquarters are still too weak. Active elevation of the neck produces such painful pressure on the cervical vertebrae that any horse will defend itself instinctively either by rigidly tensing the muscles of its back or slackening them completely.

Horizontal equilibrium is the result of the diligent activity of elastic hind legs stepping sufficiently forwards, flexing willingly under weight and extending smoothly. As this horizontal equilibrium improves, the feet start detaching themselves more distinctly from the ground, the gait becomes sprightlier and speed can be regulated easily. The time needed to achieve this result depends as much on the knowledge and skill of the rider as on the conformation of the horse.

With firm going, the state of equilibrium of the horse can be perceived by the ear as well as by the eye. At the walk one should distinctly hear four footfalls of equal intensity at perfectly regular intervals; at the trot, two; at the canter, three. A blatant sign of faulty equilibrium is the clicking sound of iron striking iron produced by a horse that forges at the trot; it means that the overloaded forefeet remain on the ground for too long a time, and that the insufficiently loaded hind feet over-engage. Too much of a good thing is as undesirable as not enough; hustling a horse by means of exaggerated use of seat and legs throws the weight on to the shoulders. Forging is simply a sign of bad riding and it is unnecessary to explain how to correct the fault.

On firm going, the sound of the steps of different horses can also be detected. Some horses trample, others skip. This is not just a question of equilibrium, as is often said, but of a different degree of suppleness and of elasticity of hind joints. The same applies to humans; the firm treading of the farm labourer makes more noise than the airy stepping of the ballerina.

A horse trained to move in horizontal equilibrium, has a spring in its step and does not make much noise when it trots.

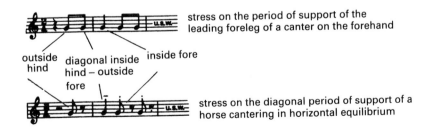

stress on the period of support of the leading foreleg of a canter on the forehand

outside hind   diagonal inside hind – outside fore   inside fore

stress on the diagonal period of support of a horse cantering in horizontal equilibrium

At the canter, with the three periods of support of outside hind, inside hind and outside fore together, inside fore, the stress should be on the second period of support of inside hind and outside fore. If the horse canters on the forehand, the stress will be on the third period of support of the leading foreleg.

The different stresses are a clear indication in the first case of faulty, in the second case of correct equilibrium.

4 Balance

The previous chapter discussed equilibrium between the front end and the back end of the horse. In German, when we say balance, we refer to lateral equilibrium.

Observed from the front or the rear, a horse moving on a straight line can be divided from head to tail into two roughly symmetrical parts by an imaginary vertical plane. It is said that a horse is straight when, on straight lines, on bends and on circles, each hind foot steps exactly in the trace of the ipsilateral (on the same side of the body) forefoot. When it comes to circling and bending, this is a paradox. To circle and turn correctly on one track, a horse must incurvate to a degree corresponding to the circumference of the circle; it cannot therefore be straight. To a layman the statement that straightness implies incurvation seems illogical; paradoxes of this kind are not helpful to a better understanding of the art. However, this apparent contradiction will be discussed later.

In motion the horse has to preserve the balance of the total mass – which includes that of the rider – by continually re-establishing a secure base of support. At speeds higher than the walk in turns and on circles it must oppose the effect of centrifugal force by putting more weight on its inside legs.

Lateral balance depends largely on a sufficiently wide base of support, though also on the strength of the legs. In motion, the difficulty of balance on a narrow base of support increases as the number of feet on the ground are reduced.

Horses, like us, are endowed by nature with a sense of balance which enables them instinctively to compensate by movement any significant lateral displacement of their centre of gravity and to establish a new base of support. The inborn sense of balance of individuals varies in equines as well as humans but it can be considerably improved by persevering with exercises of progressive difficulty.

Quick reactions and agility are an important condition of balance, and these qualities can be developed in horses to a high degree by a sound dressage education.

Conformation also plays an important role and it is from the point of view of balance as well as equilibrium that horses of a 'rectangular format', with a relatively low centre of gravity and a relatively broad base of support, are preferable for riding than leggy, base narrow, small-hooved horses of a 'square' format.

The presence of a rider on its back heightens the centre of gravity of the combined mass and complicates the problem of balance; the most important factor of balance is the rider's seat. To stay under the load of an unsteady rider the horse has to make exaggeratedly ample lateral displacements of its centre of gravity which cause it to sway or to step wide behind.

An imperfectly poised rider will never be able to feel and counteract quickly a precarious state of balance of the horse or deviations from the straight course and will never be able to execute accurately the various figures of the manege prescribed in dressage tests. On the other hand, exemplary voltes and a perfectly correct piaffer demonstrate convincingly the absolute correctness of the rider, at least during the execution of those particular movements, for when a state of balance has been established, it still has to be carefully preserved; it can be disturbed or jeopardized at any moment by an erratic movement of the rider.

Perfect balance

The rider can certainly help and teach the horse to achieve and maintain a secure state of balance by teaching it to move straight on straight lines and circles, or, to put it more accurately, by directing it correctly on such courses, but only on condition that he has developed a good sense of balance himself. If his own sense of balance is so poorly developed that he has to depend on grip or the reins to stay on he will never achieve entirely satisfactory results.

It is too much to expect a horse to establish and preserve a steady state of balance at the trot if its rider does not make a serious effort to sit up and sit still, especially if the horse is base narrow. In this case, it is equally essential to get the horse to move actively; speed is an important factor of balance.

One would imagine that a broad-chested horse would be better able to maintain its balance than a narrow horse. This may be so at the halt, when it is easy for the rider to sit still. However in movement the centre of gravity has to be constantly displaced from side to side so that it can be

Precarious balance
of a horse performing
a faulty passage

supported alternately by one forelimb and then the other,
and the swaying is all the more pronounced if the distance
of the shoulders from the central longitudinal axis is
greater. Schooling can do little to improve the balance of a
horse with this sort of conformation.

It is difficult enough to ride straight (hind hooves
treading exactly in the traces of fore hooves) when a horse is
well made. It is extremely difficult to do so if it has serious
problems of conformation; one should not therefore consider training for dressage horses that are abnormally
narrow- or broad-chested.

5 Suppleness

The next concept of dressage that needs to be properly understood is what we Germans call looseness, i.e. suppleness; it means the same thing as freedom or ease of movement. This is not just a matter of equilibrium or balance. The term indicates a certain physical and psychological state. Physically, it implies harmonious activity of all the parts of the body that have to participate in the mechanics of locomotion, smooth alternation of contraction and elongation of all the muscles involved, economy of effort or, to put it in one word, efficiency.

Psychologically, it implies calm, attentiveness, acceptance of aids. A horse should remain mentally relaxed even when required to work with maximum energy.

Suppleness depends on physical well-being and mental poise. Its external signs are regularity and elegance of movement, smooth play of muscles, pulsations running through the whole system, regular snorting at the canter, relaxed tail carriage, mobility of the ears, attentiveness to the rider and silent chewing of the bit.

A supple horse obeys discreet aids without demur. It uses no more than necessary muscular tension for the production of work and the correct execution of the movement commanded. It does not waste energy on opposition to the will of the rider. However an important condition of physical or psychological suppleness is the ease with which the rider maintains the correctness of his own position; the aids cannot be used tactfully and effectively if the rider himself is not supple.

In the more advanced education of the horse, when it has to learn to move in collection, with more weight on the hind legs than on the forelegs – therefore on a smaller base of support – its submission cannot be obtained if it does not ease all tension unnecessary to the correct execution of the movement (a rigid body cannot be compacted into a small frame). Suppleness is always a requisite of good work and has to be carefully fostered at all stages of a horse's education. Regrettably there are too many riders who forget this. In dressage tests, the walk on a long rein is meant to be a demonstration of suppleness, but one should be able to allow the horse to lengthen the reins even at a medium trot. However there is a right and a wrong way of doing this. Suddenly surrendering the contact is not the same thing as 'letting the horse chew the reins from the hand' to lower and extend its neck and quietly lengthen as much as possible the distance between its mouth and the rider's hands while constantly maintaining the contact. It is this smooth lengthening of the neck that demonstrates the eased tension of the neck muscles, an essential condition of suitable rein tension.

Lengthening the neck is not an exact term because we cannot change the length of the horse's neck; we can change its outline, but whether this means lowering the neck or extending the head is a question much debated. There is no straightforward answer. If a horse tends to carry its neck low and to overbend, one would want extension of the head; on the contrary, if it tends to go above the bit, one would want a lowering of the neck. In neither case should there be the slightest change of equilibrium; the horse must maintain the same speed and direction as when it was moving on the bit.

Why can it be so difficult to get some horses to relax sufficiently to become supple? It can be because of pain or discomfort caused either by a digestive disorder, awkward

conformation, lameness, or muscle soreness. The cause of the difficulty can also be psychological; worry, fear, exciting environment, distrust of the rider based on memory of rough or cruel treatment, an awkward temperament, or a combination of any of those physical and psychological factors. It is impossible to analyse them all the so we must be content with a general understanding of the process of easing the muscle tension unnecessary to the correct execution of the movement required.

A horse can appear generally supple and still be opposing the influence of the rider's aids by stiffening certain parts of its body (poll, neck, trunk, etc.). Resistance can be due to any of the causes enumerated above; it can also reside in the rider's inability to use the aids sensitively in accord with the movement of the horse.

No gymnastic work should ever be started before a horse is perfectly calm and all excessive tension has been eased by appropriate exercises.

Simply trotting or cantering around the manege is an unintelligent and useless method of getting a tense horse to soften up. It cannot be done by driving it on and on with the idea of warming it up; prolonged cooking hardens an egg; it does not soften it. A tense horse tenses increasingly as it becomes hotter. The right way to settle it consists in first recognizing the seat of resistance, and then selecting the movements that are most likely to weaken and finally eliminate the resistance.

If, besides the handicaps already mentioned, a horse has to contend with the disturbing effect of an unsteady seat and inappropriate aids (which may well be the main cause of excessive tension), its awkwardness will be aggravated, and an undesirable trait will become a deeply rooted habit.

Opposite page
A remarkably acrobatic feat. Only the agility of horse and rider prevented complete loss of balance

In this case the rider will have to pay for his negligence and enlist the services of an expert. The best advice one can give him is that he get into the habit of remaining at a halt on a loose rein after mounting until the horse is mentally relaxed. If so many horses of favourable conformation and temperament need to be completely reschooled to learn suppleness, one is forced to conclude that their tension must be the fault of their habitual rider.

Some experience is essential to teach an average sort of horse to relax but suppling a difficult horse requires greater experience and a lot of skill and patience. In suitable environmental conditions, a horse of good conformation and of equable temperament can be suppled easily and quickly.

Awkwardness of temperament causes much more difficulty than imperfection of conformation; temperament must be considered carefully before deciding to purchase a horse with the intention of schooling it for dressage. One can discover too late when working in the manege that the animal is made not only of bones and sinews, flesh and blood, but also nerves; natural disposition can of course have been improved or aggravated to some extent by previous training. Before coming to a decision one should try to find out as much as possible about the horse's temperament by talking to people who have some knowledge of it. The chances of success in competition are poor if the horse has not got strong nerves besides other desirable qualities.

However even if a horse has worked composedly for some time, its state of mental and muscular tension, like its state of equilibrium and balance, can change in a flash if its senses are suddenly assaulted by an unpredictable event.

Tranquillity is an inborn and valuable trait of many horses, but they are not always endowed with other above average qualities. The brilliance of top performers is very much the result of infusion of thoroughbred blood; their sensitivity is a great asset, but they often can be easily irritated by outside influences; there are, alas, no unmixed blessings in this world.

Irritability however is not always inherent to temperament; it is often the result of early training. A horseman should sympathize with a young horse that has enjoyed unrestricted freedom of movement during the first years of its life, and suddenly has to accept the feeling of a bit in its mouth, a saddle on its back, a girth round its belly, side reins, the sight of the lungeing whip – and finally the weight of a rider. Even if the trainer is considerate and proceeds with caution, every item of the tack must initially produce some discomfort. But if the trainer is unsympathetic, rough or merely incompetent, if the tack does not fit or is badly adjusted, if the bridle and bit are carelessly pulled over the ears, the saddle slammed on, the girth and side reins tightened excessively, the horse will inevitably start its education in a state of undesirably high mental and physical tension. At the mere sight of the tack a frightened horse may try to run away or may react violently in self-defence. On the lunge it will either rush or move with reluctance, refuse to move at all, turn round suddenly, buck or rear. Unsympathetic handling in the earliest stages of preparation for work imprint strongly on the horse's mind an association between gear and physical discomfort. First impressions made on horses, as with humans, are not easily eradicated.

Friskiness and disobedience are perfectly natural when healthy, mettlesome young horses feel the fresh air after hours of confinement in the stable; they soom calm down and their antics should not be confused with the furious opposition that can be put up by horses that have been roughly treated.

Subsequently a horse will also understandably defend

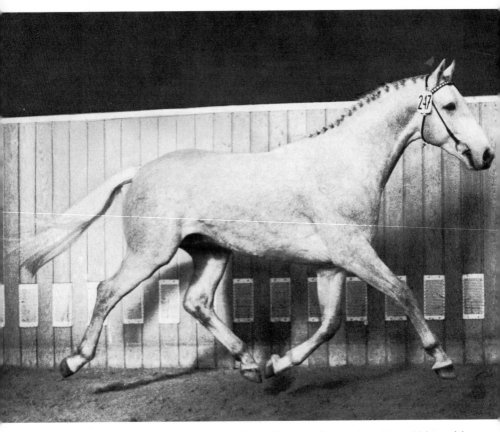

Flat trot of a young stallion of excellent conformation; it could be said to be almost a medium trot, were it not for the fact that the hindquarters do not provide sufficient support

itself if the first mounting lessons and the first lessons in learning to move with a rider astride are not attended by prudence and great calm. Every horse will at first be worried by the strange sensation of carrying weight, but the sensitive animal that is suitable for sport needs to be treated with special care. If a horse moves off as soon as the rider puts his foot in the stirrup or settles in the saddle, it shows that its previous experience of the whole process

Extended trot of an accomplished dressage horse. The activity of the powerful hindquarters and the elasticity of all their joints permit not only optimum speed and lightness of the forehand but also immediate, fluent transition to collection in response to the lightest of aids

has been a very unpleasant one. An agile person can jump onto an apprehensive horse as if it were a moving bus, but in doing so he is liable to increase the horse's nervousness. Teaching the horse to stand still and mounting slowly is the best way of getting it to ease its tense back muscles before the beginning of a lesson. It will understandably stiffen or try to escape if it has learnt to defend itself against the expected shock to its system of the hard impact

Tense trot, ineffective aids

of the rider's weight. If it does try to escape, and is checked rudely, it protects itself by stiffening its poll, its neck and its hindquarters. Mounting hastily does not save time; it just makes the suppling process more difficult and lengthier than it need be.

An inexperienced horse of equable disposition and suitable conformation will quickly recover its composure under an experienced rider who understands how to regain and preserve its trust (an inexperienced or incompetent rider should never attempt to break in any horse). Young horses that have been sensibly prepared submit willingly to being saddled and bridled, stand perfectly still while being mounted, remain calm when asked to move

on and make efficient use of their forces during movement. Their confidence increases with maturity and they
eventually come out of the stable ready to start work in a
comfortable physical and mental state. Their joints,
stiffened by hours of inactivity, can be eased after only a
few minutes of quiet exercise and the suppleness achieved
by previous work is quickly restored. Their tranquillity
amazes the unfortuante riders who always have to put up
with the antics of a fresh horse before they can start work.
It is an established fact that this tranquillity is due mostly
to sympathetic early training.

Suppleness is as much the consequence of rational
training as of an inborn mental and physical tendency; it is
an absolutely essential condition of purity of movement.
However, suppleness or freedom of movement does not
imply freedom of constraint of any kind or a considerable
departure from discipline, fitness, firmness, etc. The
difference between suppleness and unconstraint is perhaps
more easily understood by comparing the behaviour of
humans and equines.

A shuffling layabout is unconstrained, but he is not
supple; he is lax and undisciplined. A fencer or dancer who
walks with a springy step is supple but he is fit and
disciplined. A tired dray horse dragged along by the
weight of its head and neck is unconstrained but it is not
supple. A properly ridden dressage horse works with
energy but without wasting effort; it is limber and light on
its feet. It is supple, it moves with ease.

Unconstraint implies minimum possible effort. Suppleness means efficient utilization of forces, rhythmical,
smooth alternating contraction and easing of many
muscles, constant readiness for action; it is an absolute
condition of performance.

6 Contact and Rein Tension

Contact is the tension of both reins and is just sufficient to enable the hands of the rider to communicate with the mouth of the horse. On the other hand, rein tension as we understand it in dressage, is a steady – though variable depending on speed – degree of tension, transmitted along the horse's neck and back to the hindquarters, which allows the rider to control their propulsive action with utmost precision. In the earliest stages of schooling, contact should be as light as possible but a more tangible and elastic rein tension can be established when the horse starts carrying itself better as a result of the engagement and energetic activity of its hind legs. However, no rein tension is possible before the horse has learnt to relax the muscles of its neck and jaw, before it chews the bit noiselessly and regularly, before its back muscles function correctly and before it has lengthened its topline. When it puts an elastic tension on the reins of its own accord, the horse is said to be 'on the bit'. It is on the bit when it allows its nose to drop near to the vertical and the bit to rest quietly on the bars of the mouth; the reins should form an approximate right angle with the bars of the mouth; their effects can then extend quickly and surely to the hindquarters.

A horse strolling across country on a loose rein is not on the bit; neither is the excited racehorse fighting to escape the restraint of the reins; nor the hunter boring on the bit with its nose to the ground, nor the show-jumper tearing over obstacles with its head thrown high. It is only when it

Horse is above the bit, set at the poll and rigid in its back; a not uncommon combination of serious faults

is on the bit that a horse's speed and direction can be controlled with ease and precision. Hence 'rein tension' and 'on the bit' are the same thing. The horse should remain on the bit at all speeds, but being 'on the bit' does not necessarily imply collection as some riders believe.

A suitable rein tension is not the same thing as an invariable rein tension. There are different degrees of suitable tension which are dependent on the speed, the conformation of the horse, the stage of its education and its state of equilibrium. Essential conditions of tension are a properly fitted and adjusted bridle, a mild bit of the right size, good natural gaits and, last but not least, the steadiness of the rider's hands – which depends of course, on the correctness of his seat. A rider who does not have an independent seat cannot have independent and feeling hands. If a horse does not go on the bit, look at the rider, he is more often at fault than the horse.

Even a naturally talented rider needs years of conscientious effort to develop a supple seat independent of grip, and to learn to co-ordinate the effects of weight, legs and hands. But only when he has achieved perfect independence of seat and hands can he hope for honourable results in competition. Placing in competition is less significant than marks; one can win in competition with an average of four marks if one is the best of a mediocre bunch.

A horse with some serious weakness of conformation will always refuse to accept a correct rein tension either by boring on the bit or coming above, behind or off the bit. A punctilious examination of conformation is not necessary however; some weak points can be compensated for by other strong points. One must develop an eye for good conformation but powerful, efficient movement is not always associated with a beautiful exterior.

For example, if a horse's head is set rather high (occiput higher than atlas), sufficient flexion at the poll could be difficult to obtain; the defect can be counteracted to some extent by a well-shaped neck and head, with a wide space within the lower jaw. It would be even more objectionable if the horse had a small jaw, a neck set on too low or an upside down neck. Powerful, angled hind legs, capable of carrying a considerable proportion of weight can compensate for some imperfection of forehand, but long, straight hind legs would compound the disadvantage of an insufficiently sloping shoulder. Straight hind legs are not a disadvantage for race horses; they facilitate propulsion, but in the case of the dressage horse, straight hind legs enable the horse to resist easily the regulating effects of the rider's hands and to put an unbearable strain on the rider's shoulders and arms.

This leads many riders to believe that the horse has a hard mouth since it is the hand that feels the resistance, but the insensitivity of the mouth is not the real cause of objection to rein tension; the cause is stiffness in either the poll or the hindquarters. A horse that carries itself easily in horizontal equilibrium and uses its back and hind joints actively and smoothly does not fatigue the rider's arms even in maximum extension of the canter which requires a firm rein tension. It is by developing the elasticity of all parts of the horse's locomotive system simultaneously, by rational gymnastic work, that one cures stubborn opposition to the rein effects and gets the horse to chew the bit and to offer an agreeable and effective rein tension. Methods may vary, because they have to be adapted to the conformation and temperament of the individual horse but it is never by working on the mouth alone that one can achieve an elastic, positive rein tension.

It is impossible to determine an ideal degree of tension. The assertion that rein tension must always be as light as possible is nonsense. The suitable degree of tension depends entirely on the state of equilibrium of the horse. One can only say that it should be 'normal' or 'positive' at the working and medium gaits when the propulsive and carrying capacities of the hindquarters are roughly equal; it should be lighter than normal at the collected gaits, when the hindquarters are more loaded than the forehand and carry more than they drive; firmer than normal at the extended gaits when the hind legs are used principally for propulsion.

The rein tension must be equal at all speeds, however, on straight lines and on circles. In all movements in which the horse is incurvated, the outside rein is the steadying one and should therefore feel a little tauter than the inside rein which just has to maintain position; nevertheless the inside rein should not be slack (except in the movement known as leg yielding when only the horse's head can be –

but does not have to be – inflected). If a horse always pulls on one rein and refuses to stretch the other, it is not straight and is not driving itself forwards equally with both hind legs.

With almost all horses, to a varying degree, one hind leg is naturally stronger than the other; this is called the natural crookedness of horses. An equal rein tension cannot, therefore, be expected at the beginning of training; but a perfectly equal rein tension in all movements on one or two tracks *is* one of the important objects of a thorough dressage education and is a touchstone of suppleness and tractability. The horse must chew the bit quietly and regularly with its mouth closed; a little foam of saliva then builds up on both sides of the lips, and the horse obeys equally willingly the instructions of the right or the left rein.

Equality of rein tension is the result of sensitive and co-ordinated aids but also of the horse's willingness to work. If it engages both hind legs effectively and steps actively and regularly, it drives itself on to the bit and seeks to maintain the tension of reins of its own accord. When the rider allows it to 'lengthen its neck' by opening his fingers, it continues to chew the bit to draw the reins from his hands smoothly and gradually without altering its gait. This gentle 'chewing of the reins from the hand' is a very good test of submission; many riders neglect to give the horse the opportunity to 'chew the reins from the hand' frequently enough in the course of the lesson as if it were a waste of precious time. Genuine horsemen, on the other hand, understand the benefits of letting a horse stretch out in this manner after it has worked honestly for some time. They feel or see the right moment; the pseudo-experts always miss it.

For a knowledgeable observer, the degree of rein tension, especially in the *parades* (transitions from canter or trot to halt), says much about the degree of submission of the horse. A famous riding master of the last century would say to a rider who flaunted the cleverness of his horse: 'Just trot around the manege once and execute a parade to halt: this will tell me more about your horse than all those remarkable movements'. But he would also say that one could not judge a horse's degree of submission by observing only the position of its head and neck.

It is easy to see when a horse is above the bit or is leaning on the bit, but not so easy to decide when a horse is behind the bit because a horse whose nose is behind the vertical is not necessarily behind the bit.

A horse that is behind the bit is one that tucks in its chin to slacken the reins and escape control. This is a detestable fault that makes the horse completely ungovernable.

On the other hand, the horse's nose can be behind the vertical because of a certain stiffness of the poll owing to conformation, or because of an excessive shortening of the reins by the rider; this does not mean that the horse is behind the bit. Provided that it is moving with energy, it is using its back muscles and its steps are springy, the fault should not be marked too severely. In fact, it ought to be ignored if it only happens for a very short moment during the execution of a particularly difficult parade transition. The rider may just have acted unnecessarily strongly. There is a world of difference between behind the vertical and behind the bit.

There are people who say that an ideal rein tension means that the rider feels nothing in the hand, but it is a fanciful notion. If the rider can feel nothing, it is either because the horse is behind the bit, or because the rider has deliberately totally surrendered the contact to let the horse know that the schooling session has come to an end. During schooling a rein tension that borders on slackness is impractical and undesirable.

Even in the piaffer, when the rein tension should be very light because the major proportion of the weight is carried by the hindquarters, the horse must remain on the bit to show its intense desire to go forwards; it should always be possible to obtain an extended trot directly out of the piaffer.

A feeling of an empty hand should sound the alarm in the rider's mind, warning him that the horse is about to come off the bit; he must then immediately use his legs to send the horse forward to his hand and restore the elasticity of tension which ensures the possibility of regulating the gait without delay. 'Nothing in the hand' means no impulsion; it is just as bad as a listless, springless trot that deprives the rider of all feeling of the horse's movement through his seat.

It takes some years of schooling to obtain the ideal; a constantly equal, steady, soft and elastic rein tension, but in the advanced tests it is as important a requirement as suppleness, equilibrium, carriage and regularity. Until this ideal is achieved, a perfectly fluent performance is out of the question.

It is only too obvious that many horses presented in Grand Prix competition are not truly on the bit; it shows that either the rider or the horse is not sufficiently prepared for the difficulty of the test. Muddling along, albeit with accuracy, through all the movements of an advanced dressage test – which is supposed to prove the near perfect submission of the horse and the proficiency of the rider – is a pointless exercise. One may sometimes be lucky, but one cannot be consistently successful. If teachers expected a higher standard and if riders examined themselves more critically, there would no doubt be fewer participants in competitions at Grand Prix level, but the spectacle would be more edifying.

7 Straightness

In the literature of horsemanship there is no subject that has exercised the mind of authors more than the one of straightness. The importance of straight movement, or rather of the corruption of the natural crookedness of horses, has been appreciated for centuries.

Straightness does not mean absolute symmetry of all the parts of the horse's body on either side of its longitudinal axis. Neither humans nor horses are perfectly symmetrical in form.

In the sense in which horsemen use the term, straightness means that on the straight and in turns or circles the hind hooves tread in the traces of the ipsilateral front hooves. It is straightness that permits efficiency and control of movement.

The perfectly straight horse does not exist but the reasons advanced by various authors for the inborn crookedness of horses are not all the same. Whatever the reason may be, at the beginning of its education, every horse steps more or less 'out of line' with a hind foot – or a forefoot. Whether it is a fore or hind foot that is placed out of line is immaterial; the result is that one hind foot is not treading on the same line as its ipsilateral forefoot. It can also happen that both hind feet step outside the traces of the forefeet.

What is intriguing is that the signs of crookedness have been described differently by various authors, which only goes to show that horses will try more than one way of avoiding effort. Some of them move to either side at an oblique angle to the track while keeping themselves straight from head to tail; others bend their neck in front of the withers or turn their croup to one side or the other, sometimes when turning in only one direction, and

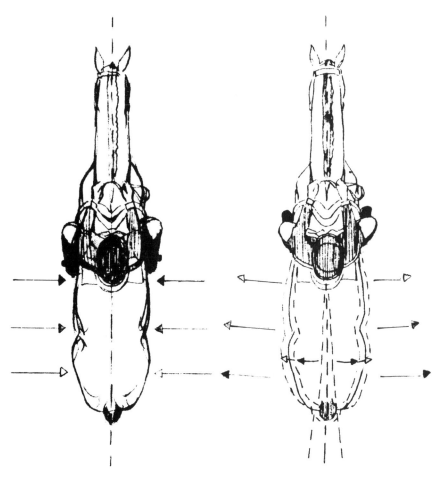

Left: The horse is moving straight, the rider sitting centrally with his legs and seat 'framing' the horse. *Right:* The rider's lower legs are too far forward to enable them to control the wobbling movement of the horse's chest

sometimes when turning in either direction. In all cases, they do it to lighten the work for the weaker hind leg. In the experience of most authorities, the right hind is the weaker one; the one which the horse always attempts to unload; but this is not invariably the case.

The degree of crookedness differs from horse to horse (with some horses it varies with gait) and is more pronounced with some riders, a fact that the rider of a noticeably crooked horse is always loath to admit. A horse may be passably straight at walk and trot, yet be crooked at canter. In fact, a rather oblique position in relation to the general direction of movement is known to facilitate the canter (which is not a gait natural to horses).

Given the slightest opportunity, the majority of horses will attempt to resort to the labour-saving expedient of crookedness. A rider may finally succeed in thwarting his horse's instinctive way of shirking honest work, only to find out that it immediately discovers another evasion. Some horses manage to trick their rider in this fashion for the whole of their working life. Describing the various forms of crookedness would take up too much space and I propose therefore just to discuss the principle of straightness, leaving the rider to find out the best method of teaching his horse to move straight.

Although it is true that most horses are naturally inclined to move somewhat crookedly, crookedness can also be an acquired fault caused by a rider who cannot feel the right moment for the use of legs or hands, slows the movement excessively, overshortens the horse or positions it wrongly in the lateral movements. 'Pushing from behind and holding in front' is often the advocated remedy for crookedness, and also often precisely the cause of crookedness. Once the horse has succeeded in disengaging a hind leg without the rider feeling and correcting the fault, the more the rider drives, the more he aggravates the

situation. Unsympathetic hands are probably the major cause of crookedness.

One can compare this senseless contradictory activity of legs and hands with futile attempts to nail together two pieces of timber. If the nail is not straight to start with, the harder one hammers, the more it bends. Is it the fault of the hammer or the fault of the wood? More than probably, it is because the wood is too hard.

If not corrected early, this dodging of honest work becomes an enduring habit that may be impossible to cure. Therefore, throughout the whole education of the horse, straightness has to be at the forefront of the rider's mind. He must remain aware of the fact that even if a horse has learnt to move straight in the medium gaits, it may still resort to the same trick later when it is being taught to move in collection.

Horses do not have the power to reason; they are incapable of deliberating a plan of action. It is purely their instinct that dictates the various ways in which they can exploit their evasions and/or resistances to thwart the schemes of men.

There are three places at which horses can appreciably bend their spine laterally: at the second vertebra (the axis), at the withers (cervicothoracic junction) and again at the lumbo-sacral articulation. If one thinks of impulsion as a current flowing through a tube, if the tube is bent at one of

Opposite page
The main purpose of work in the pillars is the development of impulsion in collection. At the end of this period of schooling, the horse, unencumbered by the weight of a rider, should be able to continue to move at a regular, very cadenced piaffer for a considerable length of time, animated only by what has become for it a constant, instinctive urge to go forwards. It is now so attentive to its trainer that, should its energy appear to wane, a click of the tongue is usually enough to get it to quicken its steps again

those three points, the current will leak out and energy will be lost. From the rider's point of view, the disadvantages of crookedness are: inefficient utilization of the propulsive force of the hindquarters (to be effective, a driving or a lifting force must always act in the direction of the centre of gravity of the mass), and ineffectiveness of the controlling aids. It is impossible to collect a crooked horse. Crookedness is frequently the reason why so many promising horses remain stuck at a relatively low level of dressage.

All horses have to be taught to move straight, and the lesson takes time to sink in even when the pupil is talented. It is, however, normal for a young horse at novice or elementary level to occasionally disengage a hind leg, or for a more educated horse to do so for a short moment in a collected movement that still causes it some difficulty, without getting out of control. No horse can be expected to work with the precision that can be built into man-engineered mechanisms; and even these sometimes let us down, but consistent crookedness at any level of dressage shows incompetent training and has to be penalized by the judges.

To keep a horse straight, to guide the shoulders correctly in the turns, and to prevent a break at the withers, it is essential that each hand remain on its own side of the horse's neck; but the rider's legs must assist his hands in controlling direction. When a horse is enclosed within the aids of hands and legs, the propulsive force of its hind legs can be fully utilized or regulated. Quite often a horse that moves with a certain indolence will suddenly perk up under the influence of emphatic straightening aids.

On turns and circles, a horse can be said to move straight if its hind feet follow exactly in the traces of its front feet; the horse must therefore be evenly incurvated from head to tail to the same degree as the curvature of the circle. It may seem absurd to say that a horse is straight when it is incurvated; a thing cannot be straight if it is bent. It would be better perhaps to talk about straightness only when the horse is moving on a straight line; on turns and circles, it would be accurate to say 'correctly curved' or 'correctly guided in the turns'.

Whatever the words used, the important thing is that we mean the same thing, although I can see no valid reason for continuing to use certain terms coined in the baroque period of horsemanship if modern riders find them confusing.

It is fairly easy to feel whether a horse is moving straight on straight lines; it is much more difficult to feel whether it is curved to a suitable degree on turns and circles.

There is the added difficulty that most horses tend to resist curving one side of their body and to hollow the opposite side only too willingly. The rider feels that, when going large, the horse turns the croup out to resist the bending effect of the inside rein; this hard side is called the stiff side. In the opposite direction, the horse seems to comply very willingly to the restraining effect of the inside rein (and thus fools the inexperienced rider who mistakes this for a sign of submission), but to avoid having to support more weight with its inside hind it places the inside foot down closer to the centre of the turn or circle; alternately it throws its shoulders out in the turn and bends only its neck. This soft or hollow side is in fact the *difficult* side. The actual purpose of riding circles and turns correctly, with the horse evenly curved from head to tail, is to oblige the horse to support more weight with its inside hind and consequently to increase the flexion of all the joints of this limb. It is by resisting overall flexing that the horse succeeds in stiffening the joints of its weaker inside hind.

Even on straight lines a horse has a hollow and a stiff

Opposite page
(Top) In the course of schooling at the trot, superior impulsion is produced by frequently alternating periods of trotting in collection with periods of extension. Eventually this cultivated impulsion produces a powerful, elevated passage which gains increasingly in expression when it is combined with periods of medium and extended trot

Opposite page
(Bottom) Classical parade to halt. The haunches are flexed and support enough weight to enable the horse to maintain a graceful elevation of its neck and head on a very light rein tension. The classical parade to halt from trot or canter is rightly considered to be one of the three most important tests of good schooling (the other two being a good medium trot and the quiet, progressive lengthening of the reins by the horse (which we call 'chewing the reins' from the rider's hand) without alteration of speed or loss of carriage. All three tests demonstrate the degree of schooling of the horse and the suppleness of haunches attained as a result of rational development of the carrying power of the hindquarters.

The position of the hind legs is not the only criterion of a correct halt. A sickle-hocked horse for example may be able to come to a halt with its hind feet under its trunk, but this is useless engagement if the haunches are not flexed. One cannot judge the correctness of the halt by examining only the position of the hind feet; it is the whole attitude of the horse that has to be observed

side, but this is not so easily felt by the rider. The inequality of tension is more pronounced in lateral movements, when the horse has to move on a straight line but with overall curvature of its neck and trunk; it is more pronounced still on turns and circles.

Riders often believe the stiff side to be the difficult one since the horse pushes hard against the bit on this side. In reality the hollow, or soft, side is the difficult side; the one to which the horse adroitly manages to deceive the rider and evade the effect of the aids. Uniform curvature and a softening of tension on the inside rein can be obtained from the stiff side eventually by a rider who has mastered a correct 'turning' seat, but, on the hollow side, it is difficult to judge whether the horse is sufficiently curved or wrongly bent and to notice soon enough – if at all – the evasion of the inside hind. As a general rule, insufficient curvature of the hollow side is less of a fault than too much bending.

One needs, however, to be a very bad or a very good rider to be undisturbed by a horse's crookedness. The bad rider is blissfully unconscious of his horse's onesidedness and does not feel what is happening underneath him. The very good rider knows that the best way of straightening the horse is to get it to go forwards resolutely; on straight lines he keeps the young horse's neck straight with reins as long as practical, in the turns he avoids bending the neck by pulling on the inside rein and assists the turning effect of the reins by guiding the erring hind foot under the body with his leg as soon as he feels the evasion.

Horses do not move very crookedly when they are ridden by a good rider who can feel immediately any deviaton of the shoulders or of a hind leg from the correct path. Thumping legs, legs in front of the girth, a leg stuck forward, squeezing legs all deprive the rider of the feel of the direction of movement of the hind legs of the horse. A correct dressage seat on the other hand allows the legs to hang easily from the hips, to remain in soft contact with the horse's sides, and to feel and immediately correct if necessary the movement of each hind leg. Straightness and correct curvature of the horse depend to a considerable extent on the correctness and suppleness of the rider's seat; crooked seat = crooked horse.

Riding a horse forwards does not mean rushing it on as fast as possible. Speed and impulsion are not the same thing. Riding forwards means getting the hind legs to step under the mass and to step actively; the lively activity of the hind limbs must always be maintained and is especially important in the collected movements.

8 Position and Curvature

In the vocabulary of horsemanship, the precise meaning of words like 'position' and 'curvature' is often the subject of debate. Judges are taught that position means the direction of the horse's legs in relation to the ground; riders are taught that position means either just a sideways turning of the horse's head (lateral flexion) or an overall even curvature of the vertebral column from head to tail, regardless of the direction of movement.

Curvature always means even curving from poll to tail. In theory there are three degrees of curvature but there are of course intermediate degrees between each one:

The first degree corresponds to the circumference of a circle of a diameter of approximately twenty metres.

The second degree corresponds to the circumference of a circle of a diameter of ten metres.

The third degree corresponds to the circumference of a circle of a diameter of five metres.

The dressage education of the horse consists of a graduated series of gymnastic exercises that very progressively develop its suppleness and agility, enabling it eventually to execute safely and easily the various manoeuvres that suit the rider's purpose. It is, principally, by putting the horse in a certain position in relation to the direction of the track, that the rider teaches the animal to move at all gaits in a manner that allows him to sit easily and ensures efficient utilization of the propulsive and supporting forces of both hind legs. At a later stage the horse may even be positioned in a manner that obliges it to work more with the naturally weaker hind leg than with the stronger one. To this end, horsemasters of the past resorted to various positions which they called for example 'trotting position' or 'cantering position' which we no longer use because they are irrelevant to our needs. In modern methods of schooling the positions are:

1) 'Shoulder-fore' or 'first position'. This demands a minimal degree of incurvation and is therefore suitable to the earlier stage of schooling. The term is an abbreviation of 'inside shoulder in front of inside hip'. The inside hind foot is made to step on the same line as the inside forefoot thus ensuring that it does its fair share of work. The rider's outside leg must guard the horse's outside hind, so that this one stays in line with the outside fore instead of avoiding work by turning out. The horse is then straight.

2) 'Second position', usually simply called 'position', involves even incurvation from head to tail; in the words of the official German Manual of Horsemanship: 'A horse is said to move "in position" when the outside aids compel it to move with its whole body evenly incurved from head to tail. Inside hind foot steps in the trace of inside forefoot; outside hind foot moves on a line between the traces of the forefeet. *(This demands more incurvation than the first position.)* The mane should be seen to tilt to the inside and the rider should be able to see the inside eye and inside nostril of the horse.

'The horse has to be "positioned" (though to a slighter degree than the one just described) when it goes through the corners of the manege, on all turns, in lateral movements and in the collected canter.'

'Position' and 'incurvation' mean the same thing (unless it is specified that what is required is only the flexion of the head). They are interchangeable words.

In the shoulder-in or in the travers position the hooves produce three traces.

A horse can also be ridden in 'outside' or 'counter-position'. It is not always understood that 'inside' or 'outside' refers to the position of the horse and not to the outside or inside track of the manege. If a horse is said to be in left position, it means that its left side is the concave side, whether this side is turned towards the wall or towards the centre of the manege.

One can ride, for example, in position left in both directions; in left shoulder-in, the wall is to the right of the rider; in left counter-shoulder-in the horse is positioned left, with its concave side to the wall. On straight lines, left renvers (croup to the wall) to the horse feels the same as left travers (head to the wall) even though left renvers can only be ridden when going large to the right and left travers when going large to the left. The aids are much the same. But on circles and turns there is an important difference.

In counter-position the horse has to execute the turns in the opposite direction to its incurvation. Its outside hind foot and forefoot move on the inside track and travel the shorter distance. The outside aids of the rider must ensure that the inside hind stays exactly in line with the inside fore on the outside track. The exercise is seldom resorted to nowadays although it is an excellent means of teaching some horses to obey the outside aids when other exercises fail to produce this obedience. The counter-position on one track on circles enables the rider to obtain, by means of half-halts with the outside rein, flexion of the joints of the weaker hind leg which is put in such a position that it cannot avoid its duty of driving the mass up to the outside rein.

On two tracks on circles, counter-position (counter-shoulder-in or renvers) is not beneficial; although the inside hind is automatically forced to engage, it is easier for the outside hind to disengage because it is not hampered by the presence of the wall. The rider has to be extremely sensitive to detect and immediately correct the evasion. By stepping aside with its outside hind, the horse can avoid incurvation and although it may move at an oblique angle to the wall, its body remains rigidly straight. The rider is unable to preserve his turning seat because his outside leg, which in the turning seat must maintain its position behind the girth, is pushed forwards to the girth by the movement of the horse. The purpose of two-track movement is therefore entirely lost and the movement is nothing more than a lesson in leg yielding – which can of course be a necessary one.

Turns are always difficult to execute correctly in renvers; even in position both hind legs must drive the horse on to the bit and too strong an effect of the rider's outside leg causes excessive turning in of the croup, in which case the hindquarters cannot effectively support weight and too much weight falls on the forehand. This can easily happen with horses that are apt to bend too much behind the saddle, at the lumbo-sacral articulation, and in their case one has to guard against any tendency to use the outside leg too strongly.

Movements in counter-position are not required in dressage tests; nevertheless the trainer should be aware of their advantages and disadvantages and be able to apply them with discernment in the course of schooling. There are riders who say that they do not need to resort to them, which is true if they own an easy horse, and if we have to school a difficult horse, it is perhaps easier to use more conventional methods of correction; nonetheless, lessons in counter-position should form part of the repertoire of the good rider who will use them at the right time, in the right circumstances.

'Letting the horse chew the reins from the hand' is another training skill that should be acquired by every

Letting the horse 'chew the reins from the hand' at the canter. Without altering speed, the horse should lower its neck and extend its poll while maintaining a light rein tension

serious student of horsemanship, even though it is not required in tests. If a horse, without changing speed, gradually and gently lowers its neck and extends the poll by chewing the bit when the rider lets the reins slide through his hand, it may not show that it is perfectly on the bit, but it is a positive indication of activity of the muscles of the back, neck, poll and jaw, and also of suppleness, equilibrium of propulsive and carrying forces, correct rein tension and generally of good schooling. There is certainly something wrong (or more than one

thing wrong) with a horse that can do everything – except
gently chew the reins out of the hand when invited to do
so. It is difficult to believe, but is a fact, that some horses
are trained up to Grand Prix level without ever having
been taught this indispensable lesson.

A high degree of collection implies a high degree of
suppleness, but a horse that will not lengthen the reins
gently, by chewing the bit when given permission, has
something important lacking in its education.

One reason for this sorry state may be a misunderstanding of the perfectly correct requirement that the horse's
neck must be firmly connected to the withers and must be
straight. Many words in the vocabulary of horsemanship
are not perfectly explicit; the words firm and straight, for
example, are often misinterpreted. It is true that the head
and neck must be steady, and that the neck should never
be bent more than the parts of the body behind it, but this
does not mean that the neck must be kept as straight as a
ramrod. The lateral muscles of the neck have to be more
or less relaxed to allow flexion, inflection or extension of
the head and it would be impossible to obtain collection or
extension if the neck were inflexible.

To summarize this chapter on the subject of straightness, we can say that when it moves on a single track the
horse must be perfectly straight on straight lines and
uniformly curved on curved lines; that when it moves on
two tracks, on circles or in lateral movements on the
straight, it has to be positioned, or incurvated, to allow it
to cross one foreleg in front of the other. Moreover it is
important to understand that position, incurvation and
lateral movements are not ends in themselves but merely
means to an end. They are gymnastic exercises designed to
develop simultaneously the elasticity of all the muscles of
the horse that have to support weight, preserve balance
and produce forward movement. Working the horse in

position enables the rider to loosen the stiffened parts of one side and to equalize the driving and supporting power of the hind legs. When this result has been achieved, the steps of the hind legs will remain lively and springy and the horse will move with impulsion at the collected gaits.

9 Impulsion and Submission

Impulsion is so often mentioned yet there are so many riders who do not know what it really is.

As has already been said, it is with its hind legs that the horse propels its body forwards. When it is unencumbered by the weight of a rider, a horse uses its hind legs principally for the purpose of forward propulsion (except in certain circumstances which we need not consider in this context). The natural movement of a horse should be observed when it is at liberty or during the first lungeing lessons. If a horse is naturally endowed with good gaits, its hind legs swing forwards regularly and energetically and are set down well under its body; we say that it engages its hind legs, and it is this engagement that makes its steps fluent and springy. The retraction of the hind leg can then all the more effectively thrust the body forwards. But powerful thrust in itself is not impulsion; it is just a condition of impulsion, a basis upon which we have to develop impulsion. In theory the development of impulsion is a simple matter of effective use of the leg aid; in practice this is not the case.

It is true that the rider must use his legs to cause each hind leg to swing sufficiently forwards, so that for a short moment after the foot is set down, the retracting leg has to support the combined weight of horse and rider. During this first phase of propulsion, the joints of the hind leg are compressed and flex; in this manner energy is stored which is released in the second phase of propulsion when the joints expand and the hind limb straightens to thrust

One of those very rare horses with hindquarters in which powerful thrust and carrying power are found in equal proportion. This enables it to extend its gaits spectacularly and also to execute the High School airs with remarkable impulsion and submission

the body forwards. During this vigorous spring-like thrust by the leg, the back muscles on the same side contract (they can be seen to bulge behind the saddle). At the trot this makes the rider feel a distinct though soft and by no means unpleasant bump at each step of the trot. It is this feeling that informs the experienced rider that the horse is engaging its hindquarters. A good rider hates a trot that feels flat and subdued; it tells him that the hind legs are not sufficiently active and that the horse's back muscles are slack. There are riders who prefer a listless trot because they find it easier to sit to, but it is not a question of preference – one way is correct, the other is not.

Powerful thrust is a gift of nature, impulsion is more a matter of obedience; it is the rider who must instil into the horse a constant urge to go forwards (which should not be confused with running away with the rider, sometimes mistaken for a sign of impulsion). The natural inclination of a healthy young horse to go forwards may suffice for leisurely riding, but it is not sufficient for dressage. A compulsive urge to go forwards is especially necessary in collection when the abnormally-loaded hindquarters must work as actively as in the medium or extended gaits. The development of the 'superior impulsion' without which it is impossible to achieve collection is not easy; it can draw gallons of sweat from the rider of a spiritless horse. The difference between thrust and impulsion can perhaps be best explained by saying that there are horses with a conformation that favours effective forward thrust – they are the good movers – but have no impulsion, and horses with lots of impulsion but whose hind legs are better designed to carry weight than to deliver very powerful forward thrust.

As Colonel Podhajsky used to say: 'Most riders think that the horse has lots of impulsion when they feel the wind whistling in their ears. In fact, it is when they start to teach the horse to move in collection that they find out whether it has impulsion.'

Horses presented in novice classes are required to show willingness to lengthen the strides. On the other hand, to be able to slow its speed and to advance in short but lively, springy, perfectly regular diagonals, at a working trot first, then later at collected trot, a horse has to be educated and must have developed a keen sense of balance and a considerable degree of submission to the aids of hands and legs. This brings us to the second essential element of impulsion – submission.

Submission is a word that should not need to be explained but it is too often understood as obedience to the retarding or turning effect of the reins. It is wrong to think of it in this restricted sense. A submissive horse must also obey the forward or lateral driving effect of the legs and react correctly to the seat. Obedience to the leg and seat aids could perhaps be said to be more important than obedience to the rein aids. In fact a horse cannot be said to be submissive before it allows itself to be driven easily in all directions, into the tactfully restraining hands of the rider, by the uninterrupted flow of impulsion emanating from behind, and before the activity of its hind legs can be determined and directed by the rider's leg and weight aids. As the preceding chapters should have made sufficiently clear, one cannot expect a horse to be submissive if it is not perfectly supple, and is resisting the *sensitive* aids of a *good rider* by stiffening any joint or muscle. The emphasis on sensitive is very important; an inexpert rider who sits too heavily or hits the horse's back with his seat at every step of the trot can make a properly schooled and sensitive horse become almost intolerably tense. If it is repeatedly subjected to such unpleasant experiences, it may never be possible to restore the animal's trust in its rider and its submission to the aids.

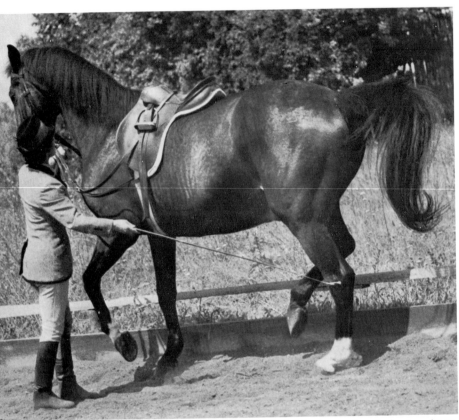

Building up impulsion by work in hand. The horse has to be taught to maintain active movement in perfect diagonal sequence of steps even when required to tread almost on the spot with deeply flexed haunches. The advantage of work in hand over work in the pillars is that one can take into consideration the difficulty of extreme collection for some horses, and allow them to gain a little ground at each step. The 'tapper' must not be used at every step; an occasional and tactful 'encouragement' at the right time and on the right spot, combined with the rein aid, is all that should be needed. Work in hand can be very helpful but is tricky and strictly for the very experienced horseman

The mounted piaffer is the final result of a very gradual building up of impulsion and submission

Submission could be defined as a high degree of suppleness. We can also say that impulsion is inconceivable without submission. The correlation between suppleness, impulsion and submission was recognized a long time ago by the masters of the classical period of horsemansip and although horsemanship cannot be called an exact science, nevertheless it is a science, be it an empirical one, and the principles upon which it was founded remain as valid now as in the past.

Passage showing impulsion and submission

It is not so much during the actual execution of the various movements of a test (extended trot, rein-back, schaukel [two or more consecutive rein-backs in a continuous movement over the same ground, e.g. rein-back – forward – rein-back – forward], lateral movements) that one can appraise impulsion and submission, but rather in the transition from one movement to the next. This is why particularly difficult transitions in the Intermediaire and Grand Prix tests are distinctly marked in dressage sheets. This gives the judges time to decide whether a horse, regardless of the impressiveness of its thrust, shows the high degree of impulsion and submission expected at those levels of education.

If a horse quickens its speed when its rider surrenders contact for a moment in the course of a lesson, it is not showing impulsion. It may show that it has not learned to move in self-carriage, that it is no more in control of its speed than a ball rolling down a hill, chasing its centre of gravity; alternately it may show that the rider was demanding a degree of collection which the animal could not maintain without suffering considerable discomfort in its mouth or some other part of its body.

The submission of horses with a serious weakness of conformation can be considerably improved by the practice of lateral movements, but at the cost of months of tedious work by the rider who cannot hope to develop in the horse a degree of agility in the lateral movements that will astonish spectators. On the other hand deficient impulsion due to serious faults of temperament, conformation, or both, can only be improved to a very limited extent and excludes any hope of even moderately good results in competition above medium level.

It is essential to recognize the root cause of deficient impulsion but this is a matter of experience. It is, therefore, always advisable to consult an experienced trainer when a horse puts up resistances that could be ascribed to this insuperable obstacle to progress. There is no ill in the world that can be permanently cured if its cause is not correctly diagnosed.

The reactions of a horse without impulsion can be confusing; some horses hurry, others, and they are the most exasperating, seem to 'die down' on the leg and become progressively more apathetic. The demands of advanced dressage are considerable and can be surmounted only by horses that are mentally and physically talented who also fall into the right hands.

It cannot be repeated too often that the execution of extraordinary movements is not the point of dressage. The aim of dressage must always be improvement of natural movement; the movements themselves are lessons, merely the means to this end. None of those lessons will have served their purpose if they do not make the horse supple, easy to animate, amenable, eminently tractable, comfortable, and a delight to ride anywhere.

Therefore when contemplating the purchase of a horse with the hope of competing honourably in dressage at advanced level, one should not ask 'what can it do?' but 'how does it go?' There is a world of difference.

If one owns an advanced horse, one should ask oneself the following questions:

– Does it move regularly in the extended gaits, in self-carriage (even on a loose rein), without having to be constantly animated?

– Does it offer an equal rein tension?

– Are its poll and back elastic?

– Does it chew the bit quietly?

– Can the strides of the walk, trot and canter be easily lengthened or shortened?

– Does it move straight on straight lines, and, on bends, do its hind feet step in the traces of the forefeet?

– Can its head be flexed equally easily to the right and the left?

– Does it obey the halts and half-halts without any resistance?

– Will it chew the bit and draw the reins calmly from the hand when allowed to?

If it does all those things, the owner can congratulate himself on having done a good job or be thankful to the previous rider; a good basis has been established and more advanced work can be contemplated.

If, on the other hand, it can perform all kinds of extraordinary movements but fails to satisfy one of the criteria set out above, the deficiency will be an obstacle to improvement and will have to be corrected before anything new can be taught. One should not forget, however, that the difficulty may be attributable to the rider rather than the horse.

It may take a long time to correct a problem but it is essential to do so if one does not want to remain at a relatively low level; it is no good thinking that faults can be corrected by teaching the horse to execute complicated movements.

Nevertheless, it is quite possible to be well placed or even to win rosettes occasionally with a horse that is not sufficiently submissive. A clever rider can manage to conceal some of his horse's weaknesses if they are not too obvious, and of course the opposition may not be very strong. The point of competition is not to prove perfection, but to compare the performances of the participants. Placing however is less significant than the score and the remarks of the judges.

Fluency should be the more important consideration. Accuracy is more or less a matter of practise and repetition, whereas fluency can be achieved only by a patient, knowledgeable and tactful rider.

Unfortunately in a Grand Prix competition judges are required to observe so many different movements, including the most difficult ones, in such a short space of time, that it is hard for them to do much else than note faults of accuracy; this has led riders to concentrate on the movements and to believe that accuracy is the most important thing, which is the main reason for the roughness and gracelessness of transitions that mars so many presentations. However, the FEI eventually came to realize that a quick succession of a multiplicity of movements did not permit a fair assessment of the thoroughness of training. And so in 1975 it instituted a Grand Prix Special with fewer movements and more time to evaluate the real quality fo each performance. Impulsion, submission, and correctness in all other respects have regained their importance. Participants in the Grand Prix Special can therefore be considered to be the true exponents of the classical art of dressage.

10 Collection

Collection is often considered to be the sole purpose of dressage; it is not. Dressage education consists in cultivating to the utmost the physical and mental aptitudes of a horse, so that it can stay sound for as long as possible while satisfying the double requirement of speed and perfect tractability. However talented it may be, an uneducated horse will never be as pleasant to ride as a horse that has been given a sensible dressage education.

A dressage-educated horse has to be efficient in its movements, comfortable to ride, completely attuned to the mind of its rider, and perfectly obedient at all speeds. Although it should not be treated like a mindless, insensitive machine, it must still work with almost as much precision as a beautifully engineered and carefully maintained automobile.

Collection is just a state of preparedness, of readiness to react rapidly in any direction that suits the rider; but it is a state that cannot be maintained for more than a short time without detriment to the soundness of body and mind of the horse. It is therefore just a means to an end. An educated rider should want to be able to collect a horse when hacking over difficult terrain, in critical situations in the hunting field, before tackling a high obstacle in show-jumping, or demanding a difficult movement in the manege.

The very word dressage, literally meaning training, is so easily open to misunderstanding that it ought perhaps to be eliminated from the vocabulary of horsemanship and

Correct collected canter

be replaced by the term education. Educating a horse means teaching it to move gracefully and getting it to understand and to submit to the influences of correct aids of the hands, legs and seat; in a literal sense dressage means drilling any living creature to behave habitually as its master demands; it is a method of instruction based entirely on association of reward or punishment with appropriate or inappropriate reactions to commands. It is not easy to draw a line between drilling and educating, but an example can help to explain the difference.

It is perfectly possible to *drill* a horse to start the canter on a determined lead just by touching some part of its body with whip or spur until it realizes that it will be punished if it does not obey, and rewarded if it does. Conversely, one *educates* the horse to canter on the desired

Despite the elevated head and neck carriage, the horse is on the forehand; the croup is too high, the back is not sufficiently active, and the canter is lacking in springiness

lead by first putting it (with rein, leg and seat aids) in a position which favours the chosen lead, and then driving it on with a moderately light seat aid and inside leg.

The degree of collection that can be expected depends on the aptitude and level of education of the horse. It always depends, in any case, on progressive education, and the sort of collection that can be demanded of an advanced dressage horse is very different from the collection that can be obtained from a six-year-old at elementary or medium standard that has just been introduced to a double bridle. Competent dressage judges appreciate this and take these factors into consideration, but what are the visible signs of collection that they look for?

In obedience to the aids, the horse retracts its centre of gravity (in relation to its base of support) by setting its hind feet down closer to its centre of gravity, flexing its haunches, and springing up and forwards off its resilient hind joints. The preliminary closing of the hind joints produces relative elevation of the *withers* (and not just of the head and neck), tension of the elongated back muscles, unforced elevation of the head and neck, more flexion of the poll, and a nose position close to the vertical; the horse must chew the bit and appear to work attentively and energetically but without showing the slightest sign of excessive effort and annoyance, while the rider should be able to sit with ease and use the aids discreetly. The horse should appear to collect itself of its own accord.

'On the bit' and 'collected' are different states but they are often confused. The horse is on the bit when it is moving with impulsion in horizontal equilibrium and applying a positive tension on the reins; the collected horse is somewhat lower behind than in front, and could be said to be more 'in hand' than on the bit. It is not easy to explain the difference, but the difference in feeling is unmistakable.

To teach a horse to collect itself willingly in obedience to the aids, the rider has to be very understanding and very patient; he must be able to feel the movements of the hind limbs and to co-ordinate all his aids with great adroitness. Skill is necessary to get a horse to work and come on the bit, without stiffening the poll or the jaw, when it is sent forwards by the legs to the tactfully restraining and regulating hand. To obtain true collection is infinitely more difficult; the difficulty consisting principally of getting the horse to collect itself with ease and good grace in response to the most inconspicuous of aids. True collection can only be achieved by very gradually building up the horse's ability to move energetically and perfectly regularly in short steps but with great impulsion, on very flexed, very elastic hind joints, with its hind hooves stepping exactly in the traces of its front hooves on straight lines and on voltes of a tight radius. It must therefore be made so supple by appropriate gymnastic exercises that it can be incurvated as easily to one side as the other to the same degree as that of the circumference of the volte. Although the degree of collection attainable varies according to the conformation and temperament of the individual horse (a lesson that a rider has to learn by experience), the progressive work towards collection is the same for all horses.

A high degree of knowledge and skill is always required to develop collection, but even experts can make mistakes in the course of this stage of education of the horse, and mistakes committed in the past are difficult to correct. Of course, he who never dares never fails, but neither can he gain much. One should not, therefore, judge too severely a rider whose horse does not satisfy entirely the conditions of perfection despite every intention to avoid mistakes.

It is easy to see that a horse has been asked for collection beyond its capacity if it drags its hind legs, moves too slowly or too hurriedly, hunches or hollows it back, overbends in the neck, or sets its poll and its mouth. Alternately it may go with a lifted croup, erratically swinging hind legs, on too long a rein, with its nose poked and its neck stiffened. Even if it executes, at the right place and at the right moment, the movements prescribed in a test, it cannot be judged to satisfy the requirement of collection. Certainly it will be impossible for it to perform correctly any of the intrinsically collected movements, like piaffer, pirouettes, and movements on two tracks.

If gait and carriage have suffered as a consequence of premature efforts to produce collection, there is no other remedy than retreat to the level at which the fault started

The disastrous result of active elevation of the neck

to show; one may have to go back a long way but there is no choice.

It is often because the horse has not been sufficiently suppled and straightened in the previous stages of its education that it resists attempts to teach it collection. One should never attempt to obtain any measure of collection before a horse has learnt to engage both its hind legs equally at all three medium gaits and in transitions. Riders who use strong leg and rein aids to force a stiff and crooked horse to bend on tight turns and circles may wish that nature had provided their particular equine with a more flexible spine, whereas it is precisely the special natural ability of some horses to bend to a considerable extent at certain points of the vertebral column that

The opposite fault, insufficient elevation of the neck and overbending.
This cannot be corrected by the hand alone; the rider must also use his
legs to get the horse to engage its hind legs and flex its haunches

enables them to defeat all the rider's attempts to control
the direction of movement of their limbs. 'Wobbly' horses
can deviate from the right course in front or behind the
saddle, and make it extremely difficult for the rider to
ensure constantly, with the aid of his hands and legs,
precise control of direction and effective transmission of
the forces of the hind legs to the forehand.

It is a peculiarity of all vertebrates to proceed in a more
or less serpentine manner. At the walk the extent of the
spinal movements are particularly easy to observe and to
feel with long-backed, long-striding horses. In order to
obtain collection it is necessary to stabilize the vertebral
column, to reduce the sideways movement as much as
possible; in theory this is most easily done by encouraging

the animal to move at a brisker pace than that which it naturally volunteers.

In practice what usually happens is that instead of engaging its hind legs more when urged on by the legs, a lazy horse will shorten the phase of suspension of the hind leg movement and hurry; or a horse that normally tends to get above the bit will start to lean on the hand. In trying to correct one fault, one produces another.

Horsemanship is not as uncomplicated an art as it seems but of course it would not be an art if it were uncomplicated.

In collection all the muscles of the animal's locomotor system have to work in particularly close co-operation not only to produce movement but also to support an abnormal proportion of weight and allow the elevation of the forehand. The visible signs of collection are not only the elevated carriage of head and neck, the regularity and liveliness of the steps but also, and especially, the visible activity of the back muscles which must act like springs strongly tensioned to support the weight of the rider and of the neck and head of the horse while simultaneously co-ordinating the movements of the fore and hind limbs. The whole body of the horse gives the appearance of being compacted within a smaller frame, but in reality as a result of correct bridling and of a shortened base of support, the back becomes more convex and therefore longer, stronger and more elastic.

The flexion of the haunches produces a lowering of the croup and compels the hind legs to function more in the capacity of flexible props than propelling levers; this automatically elevates and lightens the forehand. The elevation of the forehand must be a 'relative' elevation, rather than an 'active' elevation i.e. forced holding up of the neck and head by the reins. The degree of elevation of the forehand depends very much on the horse's conformation, especially on the articulation of neck and back. Active elevation of the neck presses the base of the neck down between the shoulders, stiffens the horse's back, hinders the engagement of the hindquarters and breaks the horse into two unrelated parts. When the rider relaxes the strong hold on the reins, instead of lengthening its stride, the horse comes above the bit and hurries. One needs therefore to be extremely careful not to demand more elevation than the horse can stand; it is so easy to exceed the limit and cause the horse to hollow its back. For the same reason one should also avoid sitting too heavily in collection and under-horsed riders have to be especially careful in this respect.

One can easily feel that the limit of correct elevation is exceeded because it is impossible to sit easily when the hind feet cease to engage and the horse hollows its back. Active elevation of the neck will also eventually impair the soundness of its back. Excessive, incorrect elevation is a much more serious fault than insufficient elevation; a low position of the head and neck at least allows the horse to move easily even with a heavy rider.

At the more advanced levels of education a properly extended walk is a sure sign of self-carriage in collection. A horse that has to be held up by the reins in the collected gaits will not extend itself properly when allowed to chew the reins; it does not relax its back muscles, consequently its steps lack scope and may even be irregular. It is, therefore, the extended walk that reveals most clearly the quality of the collected walk.

Correct elevation of the neck and lightening of the forehand depend entirely on sufficient engagement of the hindquarters. It may be necessary to use the hands frequently but only to remind the horse that it must continue to hold up its neck by its own force. The role of the legs is even more important; they must ensure that the hind feet step sufficiently forward to allow the hind-quarters to support enough weight. This is an absolute condition of lightness of rein tension. Tugging at the reins to enforce collection is not only ugly, but also useless and just a sign of stiffened hind joints. Besides which it is a serious tactical error, because it makes it strikingly obvious even to a distantly situated and not very attentive spectator that the horse is either lacking in submission to the leg aid or incapable of carrying enough weight on its hind legs.

Collection can only be obtained by driving the whole mass of the horse 'from behind' and cannot be appraised by observing only the position of neck and head. The overall attitude of rider and horse has to be observed, and a judge who concentrates his attention on details such as flexion of the poll, elevation of the neck, action of the forelegs, can easily be misled. Horses are not made to a standard pattern and absolute standards of correctness cannot be applied. One should not attempt to obtain from every horse a degree of collection which only few are capable of attaining.

When teaching a horse collection, it is essential to assess correctly its temperament and conformation and to be able to feel its current state of preparedness. Deficiencies of conformation should not be ignored but neither should their importance be exaggerated. There are many examples of horses with initial weaknesses that have been eradicated by sufficiently patient and intelligent schooling.

I am not suggesting of course that every horse can be turned into an agreeable mount by competent schooling; there are some that are totally unsuited to work under saddle. However, an unimpressive exterior and minor faults of conformation sometimes conceal considerable talent. It is surprising to realize to what extent a horse can be transformed by knowledgeable and skilful education.

Collection is the ultimate stage in a continous process of learning, and of development of mental and physical maturity. If effectiveness of aids depended on strength, any sufficiently experienced and powerful rider would be able to teach a young horse to move in collection within a matter of months. It is a false but frequent assumption. Strength is of no avail in obtaining submission to the aids; horses will obey only aids which they understand, and their understanding is as much a matter of maturity as their physical strength.

Age is a factor that is often underestimated. Warm-blood horses whose schooling used to be started at the age of four and a half are now frequently ridden when they are only three and a half or three years old, sometimes even younger, although they are not mature before the age of six. Perfectly sound, still promising ten-year-olds are now considered to be 'aged'. Owners feel increasingly that they are losing out financially, and riders feel they may be thought incompetent if a six-year-old is not presented in competition at medium level or a nine-year-old in a Grand Prix.

Since dressage has become more of a competitive sport than an art, ambitious riders want to know how quickly a horse can be trained rather than how much it is capable of achieving. Inexperienced riders feel competent enough to train inexperienced animals, and if they eventually put in the hands of a professional a seasoned ten-year-old that can neither move straight on straight lines nor turn properly right or left, they cannot understand why the trainer cannot get it ready for advanced dressage in the space of two months. The horse may turn out to be prematurely worn out; it may on the other hand turn out to be remarkably talented, but outstandingly talented horses are a rare breed.

Understanding of the horse has not developed apace

with the popularity of riding, which is not surprising if one comes to think of it. Popularization nearly always has a downward levelling effect. Nowadays, for most people, time is money, and there are few people fortunate enough to be able to spend it lavishly on the leisurely pursuit of art. From the point of view of the horse, this is a regrettable state of affairs.

Methods of training that were supposed to save time have not in the long run produced happy results; the equine work-force could not be persuaded to co-operate. Horses will counter, with violence or sullen resistance, attempts to coerce them into obedience by supposedly irresistible means. It is certainly possible to wear a horse's resistance down by hard work and to persuade it eventually to execute various movements in a more or less outwardly pleasing form, but if it is tense it will not give an agreeable ride and cannot therefore be said to be truly submissive. Submission implies softness and pliancy. It cannot be produced by resorting to various contraptions during training to accustom the horse to move in all directions in a semblance of collection.

A coerced horse may be able to execute with some accuracy the manoeuvres prescribed in a test, but a horse that has not been taught patiently how to move in self-carriage makes even leisurely hacking a torture for the rider. Many quite successful dressage horses are in fact extraordinarily uncomfortable. If, after the test, judges were required to ride some of the ones they favoured, they would very probably have to alter the marks dictated to their writers.

Proper collection is the result of a long process of education through various stages that allows no tricks, no short cuts. Educating a dressage horse is neither sport nor entertainment. It is a discipline, an art founded on scientific principles that has to be studied seriously, and is extraordinarily demanding in terms of work, perseverance and knowledge. Strong self-control and dedication are needed to accept frequent setbacks and frustration. The dedicated dressage trainer may enjoy an occasional hack in good weather or even from time to time an exciting day of hunting to hounds; but he will always have to work assiduously to perfect his art. The work can seem hard and monotonous when the same exercises have to be repeated day after day on a ponderous animal that has to be constantly animated. Certain character traits, such as self-control and patience, are as much keys to success as time and knowledge. It is not surprising that so few thoroughly educated horses are to be found amongst those that are presented in competition. But it is on the back of such horses that one experiences riding as, what is often said to be, one of the greatest joys of life.

This joy will not fall in every rider's lap; it has to be earned by conscientious work, but a taste of paradise may be offered to those who seriously apply themselves to the slog of learning to ride and who are prepared to follow perseveringly the long and narrow way to the top.

PART TWO
Practical Considerations

11 Principles

In the preceding chapters the stages and essential elements of dressage have been considered separately. The concepts of speed and rhythm, suppleness, rein tension, straightness, impulsion and submission, and collection have been explained. It should however be made clear that those elements are interdependent, that each element is part of a whole and related to all the others. One cannot say that one is more important than the other; it would be just as absurd as discussing whether the motor or the transmission is the most important part of an automobile. If one or the other breaks down, only a hulk remains.

Regularity of movement, at all gaits, is certainly the basis of tractability; but there can be no regularity without suppleness; stiffness in any part of the system precludes regularity of the walk, the trot or the canter. It is a waste of time to try to develop regularity without at the same time promoting suppleness, although it is true that without regularity there can be no suppleness. Regularity is a condition of equilibrium, and equilibrium is a condition of regularity.

The rein tension has to be the result of regular forward movement; conversely regular forward movement cannot be sustained without maintaining a constant rein tension which in turn depends on the horse accepting the bit and the rein tension. It is principally by means of an equal rein tension that we teach a horse to move straight on straight lines and to curve its body in the turns of figures and exercises; but an even rein tension is not practical if the horse does not engage its hind legs equally. We cannot teach a horse to move straight on straight lines and to incurvate itself in the turns, if we cannot get it to ease excessive tension.

Impulsion depends on suppleness and straightness. It cannot be maintained at trot or canter on straight lines or curves if the muscles of one side of the horse are stiffer than those of the other. Straightness is also an absolute condition of submission, and submission is an essential condition of collection. It is during the development of collection in particular that we realize the importance of all the above factors. A horse cannot be properly collected if its steps cannot be cadenced, if it does not move straight of its own accord, if it has no impulsion, and if it does not submit graciously to all the aids.

The ultimate aim is always perfect tractability but it cannot be produced piecemeal by working first on regularity, then successively on suppleness, equilibrium, straightness, impulsion, and elevation.

One starts to instil submission from the very beginning of schooling by teaching the horse to stand perfectly still while it is being mounted. It must, of course, have been prepared by careful handling in and out of the stable and by methodical lungeing. It has to be calm and under control. It cannot have been properly prepared for this first lesson if it runs away as soon as the rider settles himself on its back. Naturally temperament must be taken into account, and one should not expect all horses to understand in the first lesson that they have to remain totally immobile during mounting, but one can and must work at this result from the beginning and most horses will learn the lesson within a few days. Inexperienced trainers, and there are many, tolerate a horse moving away while being mounted even after months or years of schooling. They argue that the horse is still young and will learn in good time. This is not prudent; an acquired habit is always difficult to eradicate and horses must learn to respect the bit from the first day of schooling. It is not a question of age. The consequences of indulging disobedience on the grounds of youth are disastrous. A horse that has not been taught obedience in its youth will most probably always remain disobedient or at least argumentative. In this respect 'later' amounts to 'never'.

When the horse has learnt to stand still while being mounted, it can be set in motion. The rider must not sit heavily, but he must sit deeply; the horse has to learn to accept the weight of the rider. It is necessary for the rider to be able to control speed, but at this stage he must maintain no more than a light contact with the bit through the reins; a positive rein tension would alarm and confuse the horse.

The reins have to be adjusted to a length that allows the horse to move with its neck freely extended and yet allows the rider to guide it on as straight a course as possible and to slow the pace when necessary.

One may not be able to obtain a desirable state of suppleness or perfect regularity of the steps in the first lesson, but this is what one should aim for from the beginning, while making allowance for the animal's difficulties of understanding of the aids. If conformation and temperament do not present insuperable problems, a tactful rider can get an inexperienced, but carefully prepared, horse to relax and trot regularly in a surprisingly short period of time. It is purely a matter of using the aids of hands and legs unambiguously (legs without hands, hands without legs). When carefully broken-in young horses are allowed to move forwards freely in the first stage of their education they do not learn to resist the aids or to move with pronounced crookedness; they soon gain the confidence to loosen their topline and to chew the bit, and within a matter of weeks or months they can be said to be more or less on the aids.

Violent use of aids with an inexperienced horse that is physically ready to carry weight is not necessary. Tactfully, but firmly and consistently, the rider must make his own will prevail and the horse must learn to understand and obey the intentions of its master. Mutual trust has to be established; it is the indispensable foundation upon which to build a state of perfect harmony between human and equine minds.

The breaking-in and schooling of a horse destined by nature to be ridden must be attended by tact and understanding, but this certainly does not mean that one can allow it to take liberties and to go where and how it pleases on a loose rein. The animal must be allowed sufficient time to mature and no demands should be made that could undermine its corporal and nervous soundness; but progress has to be made and will be made if the rider understands that 'schooling' is education, and that education, implies a gradual, rational and systematic development of the horse's mental and physical faculties.

12 Choice of Horse

This chapter is not intended to be a detailed buyer's guide to the purchase of a dressage horse but a general discussion of the special attributes of the dressage horse.

It must have good movement. It must be sensitive and placid (this is not the contradiction in terms that it first seems to be). It should have harmonious proportions; this is much more important than the possession of outstandingly strong points which are often offset by noticeably weak ones. Its skeletal mechanism should facilitate easy extension of the gaits and also show capacity for collection.

It is, of course, a great advantage if the horse has an impressive physique, natural elegance and sparkle. It is inevitable that such a horse starts on its competitive career with an enormous advantage, but one should not forget that dressage competitions are not horse shows; they are meant to be comparative tests of proficiency of horse and rider. If, as is so often the case, a strikingly beautiful horse does not execute the movements prescribed with fluency, it should never be placed higher than a more ordinary-looking but more obedient one. It is tractability and proficiency that are being assessed and the results of the 1976 Olympic Grand Prix of Dressage, which was won by Christine Stuckelberger riding Granat, show what an extraordinary degree of proficiency can be attained by a rather common-looking horse.

To start with, the horse must move correctly at all three gaits, in distinct, light, perfectly regular steps or springs, in the sequence characteristic of the particular gait, without demur or hurrying.

It must be energetic, sensitive, and even-tempered i.e. react positively and promptly to light aids, without showing any sign of agitation or irritation. Each one of these qualities complements instead of negating the others. Eagerness is one of the most important attributes of a dressage horse. Rather than using its forces to oppose the rider, the horse must put them unreservedly at his service and appear to enjoy doing so. It must not look as if it were toiling.

It is not easy to find all qualities combined in the same animal. A horse with a very good walk and canter sometimes has a skimpy trot; conversely a good trot sometimes goes with a disappointing walk or canter.

Placidity is more important than shape; a beautiful horse may be too highly strung, too easily distracted or too fearful to remain attentive to its rider in all circumstances, but we do not want imperturbability either, because the imperturbable horse will be unmoved by the strongest aids and impossible to stir out of its bovine impassivity.

Eagerness is desirable, but excessive eagerness, though preferable to stodginess, can be equally tiresome. One should not have to spend most of the lesson time getting the horse tired enough to allow itself to be driven instead of always overreacting to the impulses of the legs. An overkeen horse can be a hard test of a rider's patience.

To put it briefly, we will rarely be fortunate enough to find the ideal horse for advanced dressage. We usually have to put up with some imperfection of conformation or of temperament which will have to be neutralized by persevering, knowledgeable and skilful work; temperamental defects however cause greater problems than weaknesses of conformation. In any case, one should never select a horse on the strength of one point, for example a special aptitude for flying changes.

Since I cannot better his account of what judges look out

for in the dressage horse, I will repeat here the words of one of Germany's foremost contemporary authorities on dressage, Hans von Heydebreck (*The state of dressage in Germany*, 2nd Edition, published by R. Georgi, Aachen, 1972):

'The horse's steps must be light, sure and in absolutely correct sequence; the horse does not hurry but shows a spontaneous, eager desire to go forwards and willingly allows itself to be guided by discreet indications on the path chosen by the rider. Its neck is elevated and uniformly arched, with its highest point at the poll; the nose drops slightly in front of the vertical; the mouth is approximately level with the hip joint. The mobility of the ears expresses the horse's attentiveness to the rider's intentions.

'The eyes are trusting and directed forwards; the mouth is closed; a slight build up of foam on the lips indicates relaxed chewing of the bit. No grinding of the teeth can be heard.

'The horse maintains a steady, equal, elastic tension on the reins, the slight vibrations of the curb rein showing that the rein tension is the consequence of the horse's trust in the rider's hand.

'When the rider advances his hands (stroking the mane), the horse does not alter its speed, thus proving that it does not rely on the rider's hand to preserve its equilibrium; in other words, it is moving in self-carriage. If the rider advances his hands somewhat more, or opens his fingers to allow the horse to chew the bit and draw the reins from his hand, the horse extends the poll without snatching at the reins to throw up its nose or to bore down on the hand.

'If on the contrary the rider closes his fingers firmly, the horse must shorten its steps or come to a square halt, and remain at a halt with its weight evenly distributed over all four legs. Without demur, it sets itself in motion again as soon as it feels a light pressure of the rider's legs.

'All its movements are free and easy and must seem to proceed from its slightly oscillating back. The ease and stillness of the rider's seat show that the horse is using all the joints and muscles of the hind legs elastically to achieve full impulsion while also cushioning the rider against the jolts of locomotion.

'At the extended gaits, the hind feet step sufficiently forwards to lighten the forehand and allow the forelimbs to reach out; in the collected gaits, the steps are shorter but the upper joints of the hindquarters must flex more pronouncedly under weight.

'Extension of the gaits must show ease, lack of haste, ample oscillations of limbs, and perfect regularity. Despite a firmer rein tension, the horse must extend its neck, and its nose must be distinctly in front of the vertical. In the collected gaits, the supporting, more loaded hind leg must be engaged sufficiently to be able to flex more deeply as the weight of the mass passes over it.

'Within each gait, carriage, rhythm, speed, and sequence of leg movements must be the same on straight lines, on circles and voltes, on one or two tracks.

'Viewed in profile, the rider must appear to be seated exactly in the middle of the horse. The topline of the horse from head to tail must have the shape of a slightly arched bow without sharp changes of direction anywhere. The withers must be a little higher than the highest point of the croup. If the horse is watched coming towards one, the hind feet must be seen to step exactly in the traces of the forefeet (except of course in the lateral movements). The ears must be on precisely the same level. The neck must be the prolongation of the trunk; when the horse is ridden in position, the inside eye, inside shoulder and inside hip should be very nearly on the same line. The rider's shoulders must be parallel to the horse's shoulders and his head must be seen between the horse's ears.

'The rider must look as if he had grown out of the horse. Human and equine body must look like one graceful, perfectly proportioned whole, like a beautifully assembled, animated work of art moving with the smoothness and precision of clockwork.'

13 Economics of Dressage

One would imagine that success in dressage competitions means that the performance of horse and rider comes as close as possible to the highest possible standard of excellence.

This is rarely the case at the less important venues, but it is what one would expect in world championships and in the Olympics. It is unfortunately not possible to devise a perfectly fair system of judging because in dressage the relative value of the performance of horse and rider cannot be estimated in terms of time, knock-downs or refusals as in the other equestrian disciplines.

Despite all efforts by the FEI to ensure unanimity of views and objectivity, the subjective element of dressage judging cannot be completely eliminated.

Over the last two hundred years, riding has certainly become an increasingly popular leisure activity, but the frequent assertion that it is now a popular sport has to be qualified. It really depends on what one means. In a broad sense a horse rider is legally and correctly defined as a person who sits on and controls the movements of a horse. Whether that person controls the horse by crude methods or according to the rules of classical equitation is of no concern to the legislator.

As a sport, however, riding is divided into a number of disciplines and nobody has the right to say that one is more meritorious than another. It is an activity that can be enjoyed at various levels. Some people are happy to live at ground floor level; others are prepared to pay more to enjoy the panoramic view at the top of the building. Can we say that the latter are happier than the former?

One does not have to pay a lot for the stabling of a sufficiently sturdy horse on which to take occasional exercise if one pays for its food and grooms it oneself. One can still claim to be riding – be it at the lowest level – even if the horse goes at the pace it chooses, in the attitude that suits it best, and will allow itself to be guided by crude rein effects provided that it knows the route. There are people who do not ask for more; they may love the horse, enjoy caring for it and sharing with it the experience of close contact with nature. They are certainly less likely to experience the frustrations and disappointments of those who aspire to high achievement.

At the other extreme, the aim of dressage riding is to develop equine agility and docility to the utmost possible limit without risk to the soundness or mental equilibrium of the animal. But it is such a costly pursuit that it will always remain the preserve of those who can afford it.

To start with, one must consider the cost of the horse. The experienced dressage specialist looks for a horse that he thinks he will be able to educate to the highest level without too much difficulty and within a reasonably short period of time.

The less experienced, but serious, student of horsemanship, should look for a 'school master' on which he can really learn, and for him the important thing is to find a horse with which he feels at ease. One cannot expect a beginner to be able to cope with any type of horse, however advanced it may be in its education. Horse and rider should be well matched in respect of size and strength.

A covered manege is essential since one can study dressage seriously only by riding every day, regardless of weather conditions. The manege need not be of standard dressage arena size, but it should be twice or three times as long as it is wide, and neither wider than 20 metres nor narrower than 12 metres.

The maneges of present day commercial establishments are frequently considerably bigger so that they can be used to conduct more than one ride at a time, or for show-jumping competitions. From the point of view of dres-sage, such large maneges have serious disadvantages. Proof of this is the fact that the track is more often an ellipse than a rectangle with rounded corners. If F. de La Gueriniere who conceived the rectangular manege, had intended a manege that would have spared riders the difficulties of turning corners precisely, he would have made it elliptical, and generations of riders would have thanked him. In our modern oversized maneges, one has to be a very fearsome instructor indeed to get riders to ride correctly through the corners.

It is extremely difficult to ride corners and turns correctly without the assistance of a wall, but the correct turning of corners is of enormous value from the point of view of the gymnastic education of horses. It is an essential preparation for two-track work, for riding in position and for collection.

Were it not for corners, the whole business of teaching the horse to move straight would be very difficult. However, to turn a corner according to the requirements of advanced dressage, which amounts to executing a quarter of a volte, the horse has to be quite advanced in its education, capable of moving with regularity in a fairly pronounced state of collection, and must be perfectly obedient to the aids of legs, weight and seat. The horse must be ridden straight to a point three strides from the corner of the manege, incurvated in the corner to the correct circumference of a six metre volte, and straightened again as it reaches the next point, three strides away from the corner.

A vast manege has other disadvantages. It is not only expensive to construct, but expensive to maintain and daily careful maintenance all the year round is essential. It is as difficult to work correctly on an uneven and badly maintained riding surface as it is to play tennis on a bumpy and pitted tennis court. In most maneges, the deep furrow dug by horses ridden carelessly hour after hour on the outside track makes it impossible to go sufficiently deep into the corners or to ride two-track movements correctly along the wall.

Besides this, a manege large enough to allow a number of horses to work at the same time can be a rather insalubrious environment if the peat, wood bark or wood shavings used to provide sufficiently springy going is allowed to get too dry and the horses have to breathe in the clouds of dust kicked up by their hooves. On the other hand, working frequently on too deep and water-logged ground is unnecessarily tiring for the horses and can do damage to their tendons and ligaments.

The walls of the manege have to be lined to a sufficient height by sloping kicking boards, not only to protect the rider's legs, but also to hold, besides the conventional alphabetical markers of dressage arenas, other markers which help pupil and teacher to check on the accurate turning of corners and execution of voltes. In the absence of the latter, it is as difficult to execute a perfectly symmetrical volte as it is to draw a true circle on paper without a pair of compasses.

It is desirable to have large mirrors at the end of the short sides of the manege which enable one to view the horse from the front when riding on either rein and verify its straightness or the correctness of its position on the long side. They also help to convince the rider of the pertinence of his teacher's corrections. An additional mirror in the middle of the long side allows the rider to check on the correctness of parades to the halt and of the turns on the haunches or the pirouettes. With a mirror facing the rider, and another in the middle of the opposite long side, he is in an ideal position to observe from the front the straightness of the rein-back, and, from the side, the sequence and length of the steps in this most difficult of movements. There is no better place for the practice of the most telling proof of a horse's submission: the schaukel. It is rare to see a perfectly executed schaukel in competition; is this because riders in general do not know what a perfect schaukel should look like or because they underestimate the difficulty of the movement?

This brings us to the next essential: for the beginner, a competent teacher; for the competitor, a coach with experience of competition at the highest level. Even a seasoned and successful dressage rider cannot dispense entirely with the friendly criticism of a keen-eyed expert. Less experienced riders, and competent riders who want to avoid the risk of spoiling their expensive horse, will also require, besides a teacher and a coach, a professional trainer (especially if the horse is already highly educated). The same person may act in all three capacities, but if two persons are involved in the training of horse and rider, they must see eye to eye on all aspects and both must be acknowledged experts.

Experts, unfortunately, are a rare breed.

It is not enough for the trainer to teach the horse to carry itself in an appearance of collection and to learn all the movements that it will be required to perform; he must first and foremost teach the horse to move correctly and easily at all three gaits so that it can be ridden without difficulty by a competent rider. He must also persuade the owner to acquire a sufficient degree of competence before he ride the horse himself: a horse that does the right thing, even in response to a wrong aid, may well be a dressage competitor's dream, but does not exist.

The growing demand for dressage teachers has produced a crop of self-styled experts with dubious qualifications. It ought to be realized that the proof of the competence of the teacher is the improvement of the horse when it is under the control of the pupil. To teach honestly, the teacher must be able to identify correctly the cause of a horse's shortcomings and to give concrete and significant advice to the pupil; the ambitious learner will, therefore, have to find an observant, knowledgeable and experienced teacher.

It is not very difficult to command a ride; it is considerably more difficult to give commands at the right time and place. It is still more difficult to appreciate the results, good or bad, of the exercise commanded and to ensure that the same faults do not occur when the exercise is repeated. This can be done only by a teacher who has the experience of riding many horses, educated at least up to the level at which he claims himself qualified to teach, and whose experience is coupled with sound theoretical knowledge.

As the German proverb states: 'No sweat, no prize'. The pupil must want to learn and must accept that the process of learning is usually attended by some degree of difficulty. Talent is a gift of the gods, and those to whom it has been given are fortunate. But talent without toil has never produced anything of value. There are many cases of riders with mediocre physical endowment who have earned laurels by their indomitable enthusiasm, their determination and also their willingness to study the available literature on the art of horsemanship.

In fact, little talent but a lot of effort gets one further than a lot of talent and a little effort. A combination of talent with effort makes things easier. However, it is intelligence and inspiration as well as talent and toil that went into the making of the famous masters of the art of dressage whose achievements have been recorded for the benefit of successive generations.

In the above list of essential requirements for dressage riding, I have not mentioned the cost of stabling, transport, vets, grooms, farriers, etc.

If we add up the cost of all the above items, without even mentioning expenditure of possibly very precious time, it becomes evident that competitive dressage riding at advanced level is a very demanding and expensive sport that can never, therefore, become a truly popular one, which goes some way to explain why so few amateurs get to the top.

There is however more to it than money. The genuinely dedicated dressage rider is convinced that the expenditure is worthwhile. He is not driven by ostentatiousness but purely by a desire to do well and to be respected by his peers. Behind the public scene, in almost total seclusion, he continues for years to perfect the image of the ideal horse. Recognition of the difficulty of his craft teaches him to be modest but does not discourage him from trying to do better. He wants to improve but he will not be hurried. He knows that he will encounter problems, but they will not dishearten him; he does not expect the way to be smooth all the time.

Dressage riding is not just a matter of learning the movements of a test and executing them in public with as much accuracy as possible. If that were the case, it could be said to be just another competitive sport which some people take up without realizing that it can never be a truly competitive sport. The genuine devotee of the discipline on the other hand is driven by a personal compulsion to establish a perfect rapport with an animal for which he feels a special sympathy; he considers dressage as a continual teaching and learning process in which he and his horse are engaged together. It is learning for the sake of learning. Hopefully, it is his kind that will attract to the discipline of dressage more genuine lovers of the horse.

14 Corrective Work

This survey of the difficulties of the art of horsemanship would not be complete without a review of ways to correct spoilt horses. It obviously cannot be exhaustive; I intend only to explain the general principles applicable to the correction of the various forms of relative equine intractability caused by incompetent training.

It cannot be stressed too strongly that the redressing of spoilt horses is work strictly for horsemen of great experience, skill, feeling, patience, self-control, and, most importantly, knowledge. Only a very knowledgeable horseman will be able to make an unerring diagnosis of the root of the disorder, and the right diagnosis is essential for the right treatment. Corrective work cannot be a hit and miss affair or a matter of luck.

From the point of view of dressage, we can consider only three categories of horses: uneducated horses, properly educated horses and spoilt horses. The curing of vices or behavioural disorders intrinsic to temperament or physical pain is not within the scope of this book. Some of those disorders may be treatable, but the subject is within the province of the veterinary profession and not of the horseman.

With the exception of abnormalities of this kind, it is safe to state that all resistances stem from some inherent and more or less noticeable irregularity of gait, which always becomes progressively more pronounced during work under saddle if it is not corrected in the early stages of schooling. In cases of ingrained irregularity of gait, resistance to the corrective aids can amount to downright obduracy and manifest itself in highly disagreeable forms such as bucking, habitual shying, rearing or running backwards, to mention just a few of the nasty tricks in the equine repertoire of defensive actions. They do however serve one useful purpose, which is to make the rider admit that 'something' in his horse's manner of going is not quite right and that he should do something about it or ask a competent trainer to diagnose the trouble and cure it if possible.

It is wise not to let the faults develop to the extent that their correction entails a battle; it takes two parties to fight a war, and even if the outcome of the fight is in the rider's favour, some, perhaps irreparable, damage will have been done to the amicable agreement of master and servant. It is therefore highly advisable to get an expert to check on the results of one's work periodically. When one rides a horse daily, one can easily fail to notice or may even condone insidious development of irregularity; love often makes one blind to the faults of the beloved. Intelligent horses are particularly clever at fooling their rider by appearing to comply with his every wish while subtly evading the requirements of honest work. The cunning horse is a much more difficult proposition than the blustering horse; one does at least know where one stands with the latter.

It is not unusual for the difficulty that has bedevilled the owner to disappear as soon as the horse is ridden by the trainer to whom it is entrusted for correction. It is then evident that it is the owner who must mend his ways and not the horse.

The opposite happens also: the horse may have seemed meek enough to his usual rider, because nothing has been demanded of it that might cause it the slightest inconvenience; it has simply been allowed to move as it pleases until it is put in the hands of the professional engaged to educate it. It is understandable that it should then resist more or less strongly depending on its temperament, aids which it has never been taught to understand in the first place. The trainer will have to contend with resistance and the horse will have to learn to obey his aids. Correct aids are to the rider what the chisel is to the sculptor, he cannot hope to give the animal an agreeable form before it has learnt to submit to their influence; chips have to fall off a block before an acceptable result is obtained.

I will forestall the cries of nature lovers by assuring them that violence or coercion are not part of the armoury of the competent trainer, but with young animals and human children alike, a system of education based on permissiveness is known to produce disastrous consequences. The horse must certainly not be treated as a slave and in many instances should be allowed freedom of action, but it must be made to understand that man in general must be respected, that his rider is unquestionably the master, and that it is to his will the horse has to subjugate its own will. Happy co-existence and harmonious co-operation depend on total acceptance of a social order by the horse in which it has rightly been destined to play the subordinate role.

In the matter of corrective training, a delicate question is the estimation of the time that will be needed to obtain and confirm satisfactory results. It is rarely possible to give a definite answer and it is seldom that the trainer will be given enough time not only to correct the fault that has plagued the owner or the previous rider but also to build up on the results achieved. The owner or the previous rider may have thoroughly spoilt the horse over a period of months or years and expect the trainer to undo the damage in a matter of weeks, as if the horse were an automobile that just needed servicing to be put back into perfect running order.

Horses however are not machines; they are living organisms with some intelligence. They may be incapable of reasoning, but their mind is capable of interpreting the signals (impulses) sent to the central nervous system by the external sense organs of the body. It is true that they will react quasi-automatically to the impulses produced by the rider which we call aids, but they will react in the way intended by the rider only on condition that those impulses come at the right moment and are of suitable intensity; if they are too strong, they cause fright; if they are too weak, they are ignored. Furthermore those impulses can be called aids only if the horse has learnt to understand their significance. We must not think of them simply as the push buttons or coins by which automatic machines are operated.

The speed of transmission of the signals to and from the central nervous system, i.e. the time it takes to elicit a response, varies considerably between individuals and, more often than not, the first reaction of the horse is the wrong one. Even a properly trained and sensitive horse can, in the space of two or three hours, be thrown into such complete mental disarray by contradictory or untimely aids, that it may take at least a week to restore its composure.

Logically one would expect that it would take a trainer as much time to correct a horse's bad habits as it has taken the previous rider to instil them; but nobody is prepared to admit this.

The trainer who undertakes corrective work is at a further disadvantage since lasting results cannot be guaranteed. Even if he has worked perseveringly until he can rely on the horse to perform impeccably when he rides it himself, he can never be sure that it will not relapse soon after he has handed it back to its owner. The latter may be most willing to accept advice but he may be unable to put it into practice. If the horse is particularly sensitive, better and more subtle co-ordination of aids may be all that was needed to set it right, but this is something that takes years to perfect. If the rider cannot afford the time to acquire proficiency, he will either have to put up with difficulties, or get himself another horse, of a less mercurial temperament, that will tolerate some false moves on the part of its master.

Certain horses can compensate to some extent for the faults of the rider; others will compound them. It is unlikely that a very sedate person will be able to kindle fire in a phlegmatic, ponderous horse. A steady horse will increase the confidence of a nervous rider, whereas on a frisky horse he will learn to hang on and to grip, but will never learn to use the aids sensitively and effectively. In fact, the majority of the horses that are handed over to professional trainers for reschooling are not so much difficult as incompatible with their rider.

Before deciding on a purchase, a rider should know what sort of resistance, if any, to expect from certain types of horses.

Resistance is mostly a matter of temperament but observation of the behaviour of the unmounted horse does not give a completely reliable clue to its temperament. There are many horses that seem placid enough when they are being handled in the stable or led, and seem totally impervious to noise and bustle in their surroundings, but turn out to be proper fiends when they are required to carry a rider. If the cause of their nervousness, irritability or fractiousness cannot be ascribed to fear, sickness or pain, then it has to be inherent to their temperament.

For an experienced and competent rider, successful schooling of a robust, healthy, unspoilt young horse of favourable conformation should not be an inordinately difficult task although it requires understanding, knowledge and patience. It does not involve the use of force, it does not cause the horse any pain and the animal soon learns to trust its rider. If the horse has no temperamental quirks, the duty of educating it is uncomplicated and rewarding. The animal will long preserve the form in which it has been moulded by its trainer and will long remain a delightful ride.

A horse with one or more weaknesses of conformation will inevitably find it difficult to comply with the requirements of dressage. Its resistance should not then be attributed to a vicious temperament. It will certainly not enjoy the daily gymnastics to which it is submitted if they cause muscular soreness or pain in some joint. Pain has an agitating effect on every horse and it is usually fear of pain that causes a horse to become tense or to openly resist the aids. Weakness of conformation has to be taken into account during the whole period of schooling; progress will be slow and no new exercise can be introduced before the horse has learnt to enjoy its work. Renewed resistance is to be expected every time a new exercise is introduced, or at the beginning of every lesson. Such horses will never give much pleasure to their rider and he should not hang on to them unless he is uncommonly endowed with all the virtues of a true horseman, but a dedicated rider, intent on completing his education, must learn to come to grips with difficult and spoilt horses. He must consider this obligation as a necessary sacrifice to the cause of the art of horsemanship.

The redressing of spoilt horses is a thankless task. Knowledge and skill are needed to do justice to a well-schooled horse; greater knowledge and skill are required to educate unspoilt young horses; enormous patience and application, besides even more skill and knowledge, are needed to reform spoilt horses. Furthermore the trainer who undertakes to re-educate a badly spoilt horse risks his

reputation; he may often have to resort to force, rough
treatment, severe punishment and then be accused of
cruelty by the owner. Interestingly though, he will never
be allowed to accuse the owner or previous rider of
leniency amounting to sloppiness. Softness strikes a less
strident cord in the spectator's heart than severity and is
less likely to be adversely criticized. On the other hand, if
punishment is deserved, timely action by a rider will
always be countenanced by his fellows who have learnt by
bitter experience that endless appeasement gets one no-
where.

Nonetheless, it is easy to understand why so many
trainers will advise a rider to get himself another horse
rather than undertake to reschool their spoilt brat.

The professional reformer of ruined horses appreciates
the dangers and criticisms to which he exposes himself. He
knows that he is more intelligent than the horse and that
he can effectively counter waywardness with intelligence,
calm and deliberation. He has so much intuition and such a
keen sensitivity to the state of tension of the horse that the
latter cannot take him by surprise. His strictness is
tempered by sympathy; if he has to punish, he does it
deliberately, without anger, without vindictiveness. He
understands that the horse's bad behaviour is not due to
animosity, but is just a reflection of acute physical or
psychological unease (caused by the rider's weight or by a
feeling of solitariness). He is forgiving and quick to
reward the slightest sign of submission. He will resort to
artificial means of restraint with the greatest circumspec-
tion, but is not averse to using unorthodox methods if he
feels that they can achieve quicker results than conventional
ones. Exceptional cases justify exceptional measures; it is
the end that matters and it cannot be achieved by stubborn
conformity to one method.

It is impossible to suggest a plan of work applicable to
all cases but experience proves that every objectionable

instance of equine fractiousness has its origin in a very limited number of shortcomings and will automatically disappear as soon as those shortcomings, that should have been made good in the first stages of schooling, are corrected.

As has already been said, no attempt to collect the horse should ever be made before:
– The regularity of the three gaits has been established.
– The horse has been taught to relax.
– The horse stretches both reins equally.
– The horse has learnt to move straight on straight lines and to incurvate equally on both reins.

Hence correction of blatant disobedience always involves complete re-education until those basic conditions are fulfilled. Further progress and honourable performance can be contemplated only after the horse has acquired the prerequisites of correct movement.

Conclusion

At the beginning of this book, I wrote that judges do not always speak 'the same language'; they do not all seem to agree on the requirements of classical dressage. However, one ought to appreciate the difficulty of judging dressage since quality in any art cannot be measured with mathematical precision. Inevitably, judging dressage will always have to remain a subjective thing, a matter of personal preference, of acute powers of perception and of reflection.

Nonetheless, all of us are looking for basically the same things: straightness, suppleness, impulsion, collection, submission; all things that go to make 'the perfectly tractable horse' that is a pleasure to ride.